Among the Woo People

KEYSTONE BOOKS

Keystone Books are intended to serve the citizens of Pennsylvania. They are accessible, well-researched explorations into the history, culture, society, and environment of the Keystone State as part of the Middle Atlantic region.

AMONG THE WOO PEOPLE

A Survival Guide for Living in a College Town

Russell Frank

The Pennsylvania State University Press
University Park, Pennsylvania

Library of Congress Cataloging-in-Publication Data

Names: Frank, Russell, 1954– , author.
Title: Among the Woo people : a survival guide for living in a college town / Russell Frank.
Description: University Park, Pennsylvania : The Pennsylvania State University Press, [2017] | "Keystone books."
Summary: "A humorous account of life in State College, Pennsylvania. Includes reflections on undergraduate life, intercollegiate sports, teaching at Penn State, and the pleasures and frustrations of living in a college town"—Provided by publisher.
Identifiers: LCCN 2017023433 | ISBN 9780271079714 (pbk. : alk. paper)
Subjects: LCSH: State College (Pa.)—Humor. | College students—Humor. | Pennsylvania State University—Humor. | American wit and humor.
Classification: LCC PN6231.S728 F73 2017 | DDC 974.8/53—dc23
LC record available at https://lccn.loc.gov/2017023433

Published by The Pennsylvania State University Press, University Park, PA 16802–1003

The Pennsylvania State University Press is a member of the Association of American University Presses.

It is the policy of The Pennsylvania State University Press to use acid-free paper. Publications on uncoated stock satisfy the minimum requirements of American National Standard for Information Sciences—Permanence of Paper for Printed Library Material, ANSI Z39.48–1992.

This book is printed on paper that contains 30% post-consumer waste.

To Sylvie, Rosa, and Ethan,
the three children I raised among
the Woo people.

Contents

Acknowledgments

I have many people to thank, beginning with the *Union Democrat* in Sonora, where managing editor Sally Scott and the late publisher Harvey McGee took a chance on me despite the fact that I had no experience or training whatsoever. Chris Bateman was the city editor at the time; if he was ever horrified by my ignorance of basic journalistic practices and precepts, he expressed it in the nicest possible way.

At the *Modesto Bee*, where I served my column-writing apprenticeship, I enjoyed a warm relationship with Metro editors Dick LeGrand and Bob White, and had the pleasure of working alongside the late Ron Delacy, whose ability to sift through gobbledygook and extraneous matter to get at the heart of a story was unsurpassed.

Jim Moss was the publisher and Cecil Bentley the executive editor who decided I would make a good features editor at the *Centre Daily Times*. Lou Heldman followed Moss, and John Winn Miller followed Bentley. All were good people to work for and with. I also worked closely with city editor Becky Bennett, and must thank copy editors Jill Bedford and the late Julie Brink for proofing my columns, writing headlines for them, and placing them on the page.

Paul Carty, then the editorial page editor of the *CDT*, helped me get my foot in the door at Penn State. He had been teaching newswriting as an adjunct, and when he took a semester off, he recommended that I replace him. That led to an invitation to apply for a tenure-track in the College of Communications from Associate Dean Jeremy Cohen and a job offer from Dean Terri Brooks. I am particularly grateful to Brooks's successors, Doug Anderson and Marie Hardin, and to my department heads Ford Risley (now associate dean) and Russ Eshleman, for their willingness to regard column writing as part of my professional identity.

So many of my colleagues at Penn State and friends in State College have inspired me with their conversation or encouraged me with their kind responses to my writings. I thank them all but would like to single out Dorn Hetzel and Kevin Hagopian as particularly close confidantes; Tony Barbieri and Gene Foreman for their wise counsel on all things journalistic; Matt McAllister for boosting my readership, unasked, through social media; Joe Selden and Katie O'Toole for nagging me to gather my columns into a book; and Samar Farage and Sajay Samuel for being the warmest and most welcoming people I have ever known.

My debts of gratitude at StateCollege.com begin with Mike Poorman, who approached me about writing for the site, and publisher Dan Myers. I would also like to thank a succession of editors: Geoff Rushton, Zach Berger, Steve Bauer, Michael Garrett, Michele Marchetti, and Adam Smeltz.

At the Penn State University Press, I am enormously grateful to editor-in-chief Kendra Boileau, who was receptive to the idea of a collection of my columns and who then shepherded the book through the publication process.

A special thank you goes to cover artist Hallie Bateman, whom I have known since the day she was born. When Hallie was little, she played a brilliantly imaginative game that began like this: "Let's pretend we're two little girls, ok?" The second little girl was my daughter Rosa. These days Hallie's brilliantly imaginative art and writing appears in the *New Yorker*, the *New York Times Magazine*, the *Awl*, and elsewhere.

Finally, there's family. My father, Herman Frank, who died in 2014 at the age of ninety-six, and my mother, Nettie Frank, who died in 2011 at the age of eighty-nine, hover over this project like tutelary spirits. Meryl Harari and Wendy Franklin, in addition to being loving big sisters, have been staunch allies. Here I must also include Michael Yonchenko and Heidi Evans, whom I have known so long that they would be considered common-law family if there were such a thing.

Sylvie, Rosa, and Ethan were eight, five, and one when we moved to State College. Now all three are out of college. Sylvie is married. My wife, Han Wingate, says adult children are the best-kept secret of parenthood. I concur, especially about my three and her two, Schuyler Wingate Lindberg and Hana Wingate Lindberg. Early on,

I wrote about my kids a lot: little ones, as we all know, can be pretty funny, and parenthood, as we all know, has its frustrations. As they got older, though, I had to respect their privacy. They may not have been reading what I wrote about them, but, they were discomfited to learn, their teachers and their friends' parents often were. I couldn't blame them for opting out, though I was sorry to lose so much good material. After all, the triumphs, trials, and tribulations of middle school and high school are every bit as interesting as those of the elementary school years. Occasionally, they granted me permission to violate the no-kids rule, usually in exchange for my participation in something I didn't particularly want to do. The aging-out factor explains why Ethan appears most, and Sylvie appears least. I hope none of them mind reading about some of their less angelic moments in these pages.

Of Han, I will only say that I am grateful every day for her presence in my life.

Introduction

"We'll Take It"

In the summer of 1995, I called a friend who lives in Harrisburg, Pennsylvania.

"What can you tell me about State College?" I asked him.

"It's a lovely, peaceful, happy place," he said.

I pictured green hills, tree-lined streets, my cherry-cheeked children playing in autumn leaves and winter snows.

"OK, what's wrong with it?" I asked. Again, he had a ready answer: "No urban grit."

My three kids were eight, five, and one. Urban grit was not what I was looking for just then.

"We'll take it," I thought.

We were living in Sonora, a California Gold Rush town where I had gotten my first journalism job at the local paper and my first teaching job at the local junior college. I was still reporting, having moved from Sonora's tiny *Union Democrat* to the medium-sized *Modesto Bee*, and I was still teaching, having picked up a summer folklore class at UC Davis to go along with the journalism class I taught at Columbia College. Martha, my wife, was freelancing. It was a lovely life in many ways. Since neither of us was bound to a full-time job, we both were able to devote a lot of time to the kiddies. The downside: no health insurance. When the third child came along, we agreed that one of us needed to get a real job, with benefits. Given the scarcity of opportunities in rural California for the likes of us, that probably meant moving out of the area.

A second factor in our openness to a re-lo was restlessness. Sonora had spectacular Sierra Nevada scenery less than an hour away, a lively population of urban refugees, and not much else. One Saturday night we hired a babysitter who had written the words "Destroy" and "Everything" on the left and right toes of her Converse All-Stars (we didn't think she really meant it). We rejected the only theater's movie offerings, couldn't summon any enthusiasm for the too-familiar local restaurants, and wound up spending our hot date at the supermarket. That was when I knew I was ready for a change of scene.

I applied for reporting jobs at the *Budapest Sun* and the *Anchorage Daily News* and for a teaching job at Southwest Louisiana State. I might have taken any of those gigs, if they'd been offered.

At one point in my job search, I heard that the *Newark Star-Ledger* had a new editor who was looking to bring in some new blood (I was told the sports editor had been there sixty-two years). When I visited the paper and was introduced to the newsroom staff, one of the reporters took me aside.

"Now let me get this straight," he said, speaking very slowly, as if to a dim-witted person. "You want to move from Northern California to Newark, New Jersey?"

In fact, Newark may have been a little too much urban grit, even for my friend in Harrisburg.

In the end, the only potential employer who expressed any interest in me with my weird PhD in Folklore, and my ten-year career at two small- and medium-sized newspapers was the *Centre Daily Times*, the paper of record in State College, Pennsylvania. The *CDT* (or Seedy Tea, as its detractors called it) was looking for a features editor.

Career-wise, it would be an odd move. The *CDT* was the smallest daily paper in the now-defunct Knight-Ridder chain, very much a step down from the larger *Bee*. On the other hand, I'd be going from reporter to editor, a step up. Several things about the job enticed me: The editor and publisher swore they were committed to making the *CDT* the best paper its size in the country and talked of my using my teaching experience to mentor young reporters (both men left for greener pastures shortly after I arrived). The paper was located in a college town, which had always appealed to me for the same reason such places appeal to a lot of people: they pair big-city culture—concerts, lectures, foreign films, ethnic restaurants—with small-town ease. And in the back of my mind I thought, who knows, maybe at some point I can dust off my PhD and take it to the giant university down the street.

As a native New Yorker who, after almost twenty years in California still felt like a stranger in a strange land, I liked the idea of moving back east. At four hours from the nearest beach, State College wasn't exactly on the East Coast, however. And once I lived there a while, I thought there ought to be a sign as you roll into town heading west on Interstate 80: *Welcome to State College, Where the Midwest Begins.* On the plus side, I was impressed with the fact that New York, Philadelphia, Washington, Baltimore, and Pittsburgh were all reasonable weekend destinations.

Before I applied for the job at the *CDT* I didn't know that State College was the name of the town where Penn State was located. All I knew about Penn State was that Joe Paterno had been the football coach since I was a child (I can picture him on a black and white TV at my aunt and uncle's house on Long Island, though this may be a false memory), and the team was called the Nittany Lions, a species of big cat that was unfamiliar to me. I assumed that the school was a football factory, which is to say, a not-very-serious institution as far as academics are concerned.

The paper flew us out during Labor Day weekend to interview and tour the town. The fall semester had just begun, and the downtown streets were pulsing with youthful energy. State College might seem like a middle-of-nowhere backwater to those who move there from the big city, but for us, after more than a decade in Sonora, the place had a surprisingly urban vibe. Of course we also couldn't help noticing that all the conversations we overheard had to do with drinking. Two bumper stickers displayed in the window of a downtown shop caught my eye. One said, "If God isn't a Penn State fan, why is the sky blue and white?" The other said, "State College: A Drinking Town with a Football Problem." Clever, if somewhat disturbing.

What may have clinched our decision to move to State College was our walk through College Heights, the residential neighborhood adjacent to campus. This was where the Paternos lived, though we didn't know it at the time. With its stately stone houses and tree-lined streets, College Heights looked exactly the way a residential neighborhood in a college town is supposed to look—which happened to be exactly the sort of life I always thought I would live.

I took the job.

About a year later, while continuing to work at the *CDT*, I began teaching a newswriting class at Penn State. A year after that I had a fateful conversation with Jeremy Cohen, associate dean of the College of Communications. I wanted to know if he was anticipating any openings for full-time faculty in the journalism department and if a folklorist-turned-journalist could be a serious candidate for such a job. His response: A search for a new journalism faculty member was indeed afoot. I should apply right away. I've been at Penn State ever since.

． ． ． ． ． ． ． ． ．

The other thing that enticed me to take the job at the *CDT* back in 1995 was that the editor told me I could write a column, which I had gotten a taste of at the *Modesto Bee* and wanted to do more of. I was a reporter at the *Bee*, but I occasionally subbed for our regular Metro columnist. Then I became part of a six-headed monster of bureau reporters who took turns writing a weekly column about interesting people, places, and doings we encountered on our beats. That did not include our kids, our pets, or our misadventures as spouses, homeowners, vacationers, etc. "The reader," our editor told us, "doesn't give a damn about you."

Hmph, I thought. Much as I liked trotting around with a notebook in my back pocket, doing interviews and writing about the world out there, I believed that my own "takes" on what was going on under my roof and in the wider world might also be worth sharing with readers. Indeed, whenever I had slipped a personal column into the paper before the ban was imposed, I got fan mail. Readers could relate to columns about my kids, my pets, and my various misadventures because, guess what, chief, they had kids, pets, and misadventures of their own.

At the *CDT* I began writing a weekly column, "Frankly Speaking" (in honor of a column my dad wrote for his high school paper under that name), no restrictions as to subject matter, and kept at it after I left the newsroom for the classroom. The column shrank over time, in lock step with the shrinking budgets and page dimensions of newspapers across the land: 800 words at first, then 750, then 700, then 600. At some point my frequency of publication was reduced as well—to alternating Sundays and then to monthly. In my short-lived blog, called "Spankly Freaking," I joked that the trend line was clear: eventually I would be asked to write one 140-character Tweet, once a year.

I wasn't happy writing monthly columns. A columnist aims to develop a relationship with readers. That is hard to do when one shows up at their front door so infrequently. So when StateCollege .com offered me a weekly column in 2009, I switched from print to digital. Thus, apart from a two-year hiatus from 2013–14, I have been writing local columns in State College almost continuously from 1995 to the present—about a thousand little essays, all told. I don't seem to get tired of it, though some readers doubtless get tired of me.

My first *CDT* column had my phone number appended to it. I heard from a few satisfied and dissatisfied readers, but not many, as far as I can recall. There were occasional cards and letters as well. A year later, I began providing my e-mail address. Now the disgruntled and the gruntled had an easy way to confront or commend without the awkwardness of talking to a real live human being, and they took advantage. One of my favorites was from a reader who, tired of hearing about the goings-on in my household, wrote, "Russell Frank needs to get out more often." I agreed. I taped the message to my office door as a reminder. I also heard from a reader who accused me of having "an obnoxiously wide forehead." Guilty as charged, I guess. I sound like a good sport, don't I? Don't be fooled. It's not pleasant to be told what a jerk you are.

My phone number and e-mail address appeared at the bottom of the column in italic type. In the beginning, it was all business. Then I decided to have fun with it, adding a brief comment that pertained, sort of, to the theme of the column, an idea I stole from *San Francisco Chronicle* columnist Jon Carroll. An example from a column about the mania for antibacterial gels that swept the country some years back: *You can get in germ-free contact with Russell Frank by calling.* . . . Alas, these fun comments didn't make the cut for this volume. If you're disappointed by that, by all means *don't* call or e-mail.

....

A personal column is and is not like a personal journal. Reading my words from ten and twenty years ago recalls a lot of moments that I otherwise would have forgotten—except that I only reveal what I want readers to know. This does not mean, as one might think, that I only chronicle moments that make me appear in a flattering light. On the contrary. The biggest mistake columnists can make is to proclaim how wonderful they are or how wonderful their life is. No one, for example, wants to hear about the writer's fabulous vacation. A far better strategy is to confess to your baser impulses, your miscommunications, your errors in judgment.

Although one can go too far. Columnists are the original humble-braggarts, trying to win readers' hearts by showing how honest, how clumsy, how self-critical they are. It's a tricky performance. When *New Yorker* cartoonist Frank Modell died in 2016, his obituary recalled the best compliment he ever received: "It said something I knew, but didn't know I knew." This is the columnist's goal as well.

As I pored through electronic archives and cartons of yellowing newsprint in search of columns worthy of revival and preservation within the covers of this book, I noticed, to my chagrin, stories that I told more than once and turns of phrase that I now swear never to deploy again, having worn them out with repeated use. (One possible exception: "bada bing, bada boom," which still tickles me.) Some of my obsessions are the ones I already mentioned—kids, pets, home ownership, etc. Living amid the fraternities in the Highlands neighborhood of State College, which I did from 1995 to 2012, provided endless column fodder. So has teaching at a large, football-crazed university. I wrote multiple mock commencement addresses, each an exhortation to work hard, not in order to achieve "success," financial or otherwise, but for the sheer under-appreciated pleasure of it. The fraudulent holiday State Patty's Day was a frequent target. So was Dance Marathon, or at least the cynical invocation of "THON" to change the subject when the subject was student misbehavior. Again and again I bashed student drinking, student know-nothingism, student rudeness . . . On the subject of student comportment, I'm sorry to say, I became something of a scold, though a cheerful one (usually).

I also kept coming back to the big news stories of the past twenty years: the September 11 attacks, first and foremost, and the Sandusky scandal. If there was a folklore angle or a journalism ethics issue to be raised in connection with a breaking news story, I would unfailingly raise it. And then there were the antidotes to the world's madness: walks in the woods, mostly, but also hikes and bike rides anywhere where there is beauty to behold. During the grim period after September 11, I ran into a reader who chided me for not being funny anymore. She liked me better funny. What could I say? These were unfunny times.

I seem to have at least two voices. One is my New York wise-guy voice (hey—born in Brooklyn, early childhood on Long Island, high school in Queens). Another is the voice of the quiet, poetical chap who fled New York at the earliest opportunity. In some of the columns, both voices can be heard. Aside from the pleasure of discovering what I think through the act of writing, and recalling the details of scenes that had not registered consciously as I witnessed them, I like the way knowing I have a column to write prompts me to pay more attention to the world around me and to what's going on inside my own head. Quite apart from the column as output, I value the anti-robotic attentiveness induced by column consciousness for its own sake.

. . . .

The challenge in putting together this book was to choose, from all those columns written over all those years, several dozen that remain fresh even as the events that precipitated them are gone and in some cases, forgotten. I considered arranging my selections thematically, but so many of them have multiple, overlapping themes that I gave up and simply present them in the order in which they were written. Needless to say, you may read them in any order you like.

. . . .

We Arrive.

Will We Stay?

Restless, rootless, corporate America moves routinely.

You want stats? I got stats. In 1993–94, according to the U.S. Census Bureau, seven million Americans moved to another state. If all those transplants had been New Yorkers, the Big Apple would be down to seeds and stems.

All this uprooting troubles me. When we staked a "For Sale" sign in front of our house in California in July, my eight-year-old daughter drafted a sign of her own and taped it over the pre-fab one.

"Sold," it said.

When the house really did sell, and we announced we were moving not just to another house but to another state, my daughter announced that she was not.

Kids are resilient, everyone told me. She'll adjust. Still, I felt like a rat, because she doesn't know she's resilient, she doesn't know she'll adjust.

The kids are what made moving hard. If it was just me, or just the two of us, I probably would have said, what the heck, let's go. If it doesn't work out, we'll go someplace else. But I don't want to bounce my kids around. I especially don't want to move them again when they're teenagers. My parents moved me when I was thirteen, and sometimes I feel like I've never recovered.

So deciding to move here was deciding to commit ourselves to staying for a long time. Unless it's a disaster. Or one of us gets an even more fabulous job offer. Then it'll be: kids are resilient, they'll adjust.

And they will. But how do people move their kids every couple of years without feeling like rats?

Of course, it's entirely possible I'm projecting my own anxiety onto my children. After all, they're not the ones who have to open accounts with the bank, the phone company, the electric company, the heating oil company, and the insurance company.

A year ago I interviewed poet Philip Levine, who had just retired from teaching at Fresno State University. Since Fresno, California, will never be mistaken for the garden spot of the world, I asked him if he was going to live someplace else.

"Are you crazy?" he exclaimed. "And give up my doctor, my dentist, my mechanic?"

Since I have now given up my own health and car care specialists, I reckon I am crazy.

Leaving people is the bad part about moving. The good part is sloughing everything else. Gleefully I tossed entire file cabinets full of lecture notes from Philosophy 1 and love letters from Girlfriend 1 into the trash. One by one, I turned in keys to offices and PO Boxes, discarded keys to old bike locks, junked cars, and lost luggage.

Best of all was the tying up of loose ends, the snipping of ties. The responsibilities of the old life had been fulfilled. The responsibilities of the new life had yet to be assumed. I was a washed blackboard, a computer purged of old files and brimming with memory.

To really get that giddy, almost invisible, between-lives feeling, though, would have required greater ruthlessness. The mover's motto is: "When in doubt, throw it out." But there were moments during the packing process when, succumbing to sentimentality, I perused file folders item by item, pausing to read and reminisce. And back in the box the items went, some to make their third cross-country trip.

Such lapses are more of a storage problem than a money problem. The furniture posed a money problem. When you hire a mover, you pay by the pound, so it's tempting to jettison everything or at least, everything you do not love.

Take our sofa, which did fine for several decades when it lived at my wife's grandmother's house, but has suffered grievously from jumping and felt-tip pen wielding children in the few years it has lived with us. Why spend a couple hundred bucks moving a shabby couch?

Because, runs the counterargument, couchless we would either have to buy a couch right away or live in a house that wouldn't look like we really lived there. Moving is expensive and disorienting enough. If moving crummy stuff three thousand miles would make us physically and emotionally comfortable, it was probably worth it.

Any day now, our stuff will arrive. In the meantime, anybody got a can opener? A friend for my daughter? A good mechanic?

"We're About Beer"

MAY 5, 1996

Are they gone? Is it safe to take out the earplugs? Herewith my six-month report on life among the frat houses:

Let me say that I did not go into this neighborhood blind. In debating whether to live in the quadrangle bound by College Avenue, Allen Street, University Drive, and Easterly Parkway, there was a positive and a negative.

The positive: walking distance to downtown and campus.

The negative: hearing distance of the frats.

Much as the biggest New York City bashers are people who have never been there, the direst warnings about fraternizing with the frat boys came from people who did not live in the neighborhood. The rocking and rolling will be constant, they said. Beery louts will relieve themselves in your rose bushes. Their trash will litter your lawn and driveway.

The consensus around the neighborhood, however, was that "it used to be a lot worse." Nowadays, my future neighbors said, the Greeks are going out of their way to be good neighbors, even offering to shovel your walk, though a couple people warned me that such offers signal an upcoming revel.

It's only bad—and by bad the neighbors meant noisy—five or six times a year. Even then, they said, the frats are pretty good about toning it down at 11:00 P.M. When they're not so good, the cops are happy to remind them of their neighborly obligations.

Sounded bearable to me: if I wanted silence and solitude I'd have been house hunting in the country.

Oddball Incidents

So we moved in. The severity of the winter neutralized the principal advantage of living close to town: a lot of days were too nasty for walking. On the plus side, in keeping our windows shut against the cold, we were keeping them shut against the music. In the absence of constant noise, the occasional oddball incident was more amusing than annoying:

- One week, the frat boys mustered at 6:00 A.M. to belt out "The Star-Spangled Banner." After four such reveilles, I made myself get up and out to learn more about this moving patriotic display. It was eight degrees. All was quiet. I should have been pleased: whatever they'd been doing, they were no longer doing it. But that meant I had gotten up early, and bundled up, and stood, freezing, in the empty and silent street, for nothing.
- Then there was the night the newly elected prexy of one of the frats came a-calling to spread neighborly cheer. His mission was undermined, somewhat, by the fact that it was 9:30 P.M., the hour when our kids are in various stages of drifting off to sleep, and we are in no mood to have ever-alert Bop the Movie Dog bark them awake. In a nice way I told El Presidente that maybe it isn't such a good idea to call on folks after nine o'clock.
- Also worth recalling are the Night of the Burning Sofa, The Guy Who Fell Out the Second-Story Window, and The Guy Who Allegedly Got His Finger Bitten in a Brawl.

Things got livelier after the thaw. All the bladers, cyclists, and runners whizzing past my yard made me feel like a fool for buying into the American dream. While they cavort like kids at camp, I rake. I also envied their manpower. When the frat boys want to bask in the sun, they don't buy lawn furniture; they grab a couch and haul it outside. When they want to hear music, they hire a band.

A couple of weeks ago, I took the frat house tour. Disappointingly, the tour did not include bedrooms. The common rooms were tidy, and the officers presented similarly sanitized versions of their activities and roll calls of famous alumni. The most memorable were William James—not the philosopher, but the inventor of the Slinky—and Phil Gramm's campaign manager, whose name, lucky for him, escapes me.

The message of the tour was: "We're about community service and academic achievement." The message of my bagel walk that Sunday morning was: "We're about beer." The number of cans, bottles, and cups on the frat house lawns was truly marvelous to behold.

In fairness, with all that manpower, the cleanup—once everyone was ambulatory—probably took ten minutes. Still, I noted with interest that the same people who rose to the neighborhood's defense last fall were counting down to the end of the semester and the peace of summer.

The President Buys an Ice Cream

MAY 11, 1996

It's sad, really.

Guy wants an ice cream cone. He saunters into the nearest creamery, picks his favorite flavor, pays, and eats it in peace.

The president of the United States wants an ice cream and a zillion guys in dark suits, shades, ear pieces, matching neckties, and one bomb-sniffing dog force every actual human being to stop doing what actual human beings do and become cast members in the show, "The President Buys an Ice Cream."

Here was this beautiful afternoon, folks sitting at the umbrella tables outside the University Creamery, folks waiting in line. Wouldn't it have been nice if the president could have stopped by, bought his cone, worked the line, worked the tables?

Not in this crazy world.

"Two options, folks," said the Secret Service guy charged with clearing the outdoor seating area. "Inside or behind the ropes."

Inside was inside the Creamery. Behind the ropes was across the street in front of the Pavilion Theatre.

"Which do you recommend?" a citizen asked.

"If you want a shake, I'd say behind the ropes."

He meant a handshake, not a milk shake.

Kerry Hoffman of State College chose inside.

"Is he coming in this way?" she asked, indicating one of the three Creamery entrances.

The Secret Service guy rolled his eyes.

"You can't tell me," Hoffman gathered, patting the Secret Service guy on the cheek.

Not everyone was as kindly disposed to the agents as Hoffman was. "Jerks," said a guy in a Phillies T-shirt as he was herded in the door.

Creamery Manager Tom Palchak marveled at the preparations.

"This is probably the most expensive cone ever dipped in the history of the Creamery," he said.

I asked a White House staffer if it was worth the trouble. His face said it wasn't. His words were, "It's been a long day."

Eventually, everyone was either inside the Creamery or behind the ropes. The lovely umbrella table area was as empty as a cold day in January. Those of us who chose inside were packed together like yogurt containers in the freezer case.

The Creamery counter people stood at the ready. They could have gone home, played a game of Parcheesi, come back, and still had time to get ready.

"I can say I wrapped Bill Clinton's cone," Rorey McManus said.

Tara Griffith could say she proffered the pens the president would use to autograph the underbills of their caps.

Veronica Brown said, "I'll probably talk to him. I'll keep him entertained."

And to eight-year Creamery veteran Kathleen Schuckers went the honor of dipping the cone.

The president was expected at 4:40 P.M. An hour later, people admitted they were tired of waiting.

"Just bring it to him," muttered Creamery worker Doug McElheny. "I could've been done with stocking. Maybe they'd let me go back there and mop."

When the flag-flying limo finally whipped around the corner, the cooped-up crowd clapped and cheered.

"Oh God, here they come," someone said.

"I see the top of his hair!"

"Welcome to State College!"

The president shook hands. Then he broke the law. "No mixing flavors," signs say.

The president of the United States got a scoop of Peachy Paterno and a scoop of Cherry Quist.

The president of The Pennsylvania State University got some WPSX Coffee Break.

Then they got to sit at an umbrella table while we gawked through the windows. Then the president greeted the folks behind the ropes. Then he was gone.

While waiting for the Secret Service guys to let them out, the lucky ones compared notes on the president's handshakes.

"He has got soft hands," said Veronica Brown.

Another connoisseur described his handshake as firm but not too firm: "He didn't squeeze the death out of you."

I didn't shake the president's hand.

If I could have asked him a question, I would have asked him if he missed being able to walk to an ice cream parlor and buy himself a cone.

Too Many Choices

JUNE 9, 1996

Choice is a big thing in America. People should be able to choose their doctor, the schools their kids attend, their long distance phone company. But I ask you: Do there have to be so many brands of shampoo? Does the recitation of the salad dressings have to take half an hour when you go out to eat?

I went to Lowe's the other day to buy a hoe and a pitchfork. There were five of each, ranging in price from five to thirty bucks. You may wonder how much variation there can be in a simple machine like a hoe. But whenever I buy the cheapest version of an item, it breaks. The I-told-you-sos in my life say, "You get what you pay for," but I argue that if something breaks while being used for its intended purpose, I did not get what I paid for: I bought something that has no value and therefore should have cost no money. If you can't make a hoe for five dollars that doesn't break, fine, charge ten dollars.

Therefore, I avoid the low end. The problem with the high end is: Why get the pro model when you're a rank amateur? If I'm the sort of bike rider who mostly cruises the neighborhood and occasionally heads for the hills, it doesn't make sense for me to pay Tour de France prices. And so, philosophically, I pursue the middle way, the middle price. Whether this is sound consuming or not, it keeps me from small-decision paralysis.

Loading my mid-priced hoe and pitchfork in my cart like a knight's lance and mace, I thought I was home free, decision-wise. But then, charging through the bathroom fixture aisle, I turned to my wife, and said, apropos of nothing at all, "Let's not buy any more houses after this one, OK? Let's rent."

Something about that array of sinks put me in mind of friends who've built their own homes and had to make choices on everything from house plans to switch plates. Buying just the right thing seems immensely important before you've bought it, but once it's installed or in use, it becomes background, the set on which the action of the bad play that is your life takes place. Why wrack our brains about such stuff?

I Bolted

A few weeks ago I was driving through the Poconos on I-80 and decided to stop at the big outlet mall near Stroudsburg. The place was packed. It was a beautiful day, one of the few we had before the end of May. Is shopping all we can think of to do with our leisure? Appalled by the advertising-induced mass psychosis of it all, I bolted, having bought nothing.

I guess what I'm saying is that I hate shopping. Since home ownership practically forces one to shop for things for the home, I wind up resenting the demands of home ownership as well. Maybe it's the weather. When the temperature hits seventy degrees, I don't want to mulch, paint, prune, repair. I want to hit the trail. I envy the young because they're freer than I.

The same day as the Lowe's excursion, I attached a child seat to my bicycle. My friend Joe, who loaned me the seat and helped me put it on, observed that the child seat destroyed the clean lines of my bike. I shrugged and said having children destroys the clean lines of your life. My daughter Sylvie, who knows me well, stuck her tongue out at me.

Also that day, we got word from a friend expecting twins in September that the little lads weren't going to wait that long. Charles weighs less than two pounds; Rob weighs less than a pound. They may not make it. My bike looked suddenly beautiful with its kiddie seat. My daughter looked beautiful with her tongue out.

Shrewd Observation

I also spoke to my sister that day. On a lark, she'd gone to a psychic who told her she was going to meet a new man, rich. Noting my sister's wedding band, the psychic predicted my sister would either get divorced or become widowed. In fact, my sister is recently widowed, which either means the psychic was hot stuff, or shrewdly figures everyone, even those of us who are happily married, happily parenting, fantasize escape from the present situation, a new life.

In choosing, we preclude possibilities, invite regret. I don't regret any of my big decisions. It's those little ones that get me down. Just give me the house dressing, the house wine, the house house.

First Fall

I heard four very scary words this past week: it feels like fall. It was true. It did.

It wasn't just the weather, which was rainy and foggy and cool. It was wind and rain knocking a few early-turning maple leaves to the lawn.

It was the rented trucks and cars with lamps poking out the windows pulling up to the fraternity and apartment houses in State College. It was football photos in the sports section and a friend in California telling me about going to the Raiders-Seahawks pre-season game in Oakland.

And it was conversations with fellow parents about teachers and soccer season and getting back on an early-to-bed schedule so we can awaken our little pupils without the aid of bugle and ice-water dousing and mattress tipping.

Ten-year-old neighbor Zev, eavesdropping on one of these between-moms conversations, clapped his hands to his ears.

"Don't talk about school," he begged. "It's still summer."

I agreed. Maybe if this had been the kind of summer I expected, with temperature and humidity routinely in the nineties, I'd be ready for fall. But it's been a delightful summer, exactly what we deserved after an endless winter and a dreary spring.

The coolness has been one surprise. The lack of mosquitoes has been the other.

For most of the past twenty years, I lived west of the Rockies, where it rarely rains from April to October. During the dry season, the creeks drain, the hills turn brown, and the dust flies when you drive on dirt roads: not a lot of standing water. Yet mosquitoes come out at dusk, and they are not dainty eaters. Here in Happy Valley, where it snowed all winter and rained all spring, I think I've gotten only two or three bites all summer.

It's been another bad summer out West. A pattern I became all too familiar with in the late '80s and early '90s has played itself out once again: last week, after a protracted heat wave, a storm bringing lightning and thunder but only a spattering of rain sparked grass fires in several locations at once. One, quite near where I used to live, torched the set of the old West town where "Back to the Future III" was filmed. If I were still there I would have been tearing around the backcountry in a yellow fireproof suit, looking for flames and firefighters, coming home with the smell of smoke in my hair and on my clothes.

Here, instead of dry lightning and wood smoke, there have been booming thunderstorms and the greenhouse smell of summer rain. Instead of mosquitoes, there have been fireflies, which my children are seeing for the first time, and which I haven't seen since I was a kid. Who needs the mad inventor's time-travel gizmo in "Back to the Future" when I've got such sights and sounds and smells transporting me back to childhood?

When we're done with dinner, I don't want to clean up the kitchen. I want to go outside and stay out, shooting hoops until it's too dark to see, or punching holes in the lids of mayonnaise jars for the fireflies we want to catch and release like undersized trout.

What is there to be tired of? Fall will get here soon enough. Why hurry it along?

Just as this was—is—our first summer back East, this will be our first full fall. We got rooked last year, moving into our house on November 1 and watching the snow fly two weeks later.

When I think of fall in the East, all the easy synesthetic sensations rush in: the crisp air, the slanting light. Even footballs and sweatshirts come to mind, though I don't think I've actually played a game of touch football since college.

But then I think of raking. And having to wear a jacket, and zip my kids into jackets. These are not unpleasant thoughts in themselves, but coats follow jackets, and shoveling follows raking: spring and fall always feel shorter than winter and summer. October offers a handful of golden afternoons and then comes the long, gray grind of winter. It's the cold I'm not ready for, and the lack of sun.

I'm with Zev and the calendar. Labor Day is half a month away. September is a summer month. If our luck holds, we'll have a nice, long Indian summer.

For as long as it lasts, I plan to be out there with the kids after supper, chasing fireflies.

The Big Coat

JANUARY 19, 1997

When I was a teenager, my approach to dressing for the cold drove my father crazy.

On all but the coldest days, I wore a pre-professional turtleneck sweater, scarf, and sport jacket.

My dad would say, "You're not going out like that," a statement that was just ambiguous enough to interpret as an expression of disbelief rather than as a flat-out parental prohibition.

"See ya," I'd say.

On the coldest days, I wore a Marlboro-man coat with fake suede and fake fur for the first couple of years of high school, and then a fake Army coat for the last couple of years. No gloves.

"Where are your gloves?" my dad would ask me.

What a dumb question.

"In my pockets," I answered.

"Fat lot of good they'll do you there," he'd say.

Now, fulfilling the ancient parental curse, I ask my daughters, "Where are your gloves?" The system of stuffing gloves and hats into coat sleeves seems to be beyond us as a family.

Now I bundle up, though residual teenage machismo and memories of a college course on the works of James Joyce make me self-conscious about it.

In Joyce's story "The Dead"—John Huston made a movie version of it ten years ago—a husband learns that his wife once loved a man more passionately than she had ever loved him. My professor, a great, big guy named Zack Bowen who lost a lot of weight and looked like a deflated football, pointed out the contrast between the middle-aged husband, who fusses with galoshes and umbrellas, and the young lover, who stood uncovered in the rain and died of consumption.

The message, Professor Bowen assured us, was not to button up your overcoat when the wind is free. Rather, he posed the questions: Do you want to live passionately, poetically, intensely? Or do you want to worry about staying warm and dry?

At twenty, you go for the gusto. At forty, warm and dry sounds pretty good. And so I was not displeased when for Christmas last year, my wife gave me the Mother of All Coats.

It's beige and puffy and comes down past my knees. In it, I look like the Stay Puft Marshmallow Man in "Ghostbusters." When I zip it as high as it will zip, it covers my nose. When I flip up the hood, Velcro it across my chin, and pull the drawstrings tight, I look ready to shut down a nuclear reactor.

It's the kind of coat that draws comment: "That's quite a coat."

It never sounds like a compliment.

The fact is, my new coat is dorky. For that reason, I didn't wear it much last winter. It's too cumbersome for shoveling snow, and last winter I shoveled snow almost as often as I shaved. This winter I haven't done much shoveling or shaving, but it's been warm enough for less dweeby outerwear—until lately. Lately, I've taken to heart what I was told shortly after I moved from California: Winter is not about looking cool. It's about staying warm.

Still, there are limits. When I go out in broad daylight, I don't do the whole radioactivity-suit thing with my coat. If I remember, I detach the hood. Hoodless, collar open, I look like a guy who's eaten a few too many KitKat bars, instead of like a complete weather weenie.

Then I see people—Penn State students, mostly, who are impervious to weather—wearing what my mom used to call a fall jacket, as opposed to a winter coat. Or I see someone riding a bicycle, which in weather like this looks about as appealing as having someone put a tray full of ice cubes down my clothes. And again I feel ashamed of my lack of cold weather hardihood. I see myself as this old guy who should be wearing a tweedy little fedora like the ones my dad used to wear before he moved to Florida and took up ball caps and Greek fishermen's caps.

At night though, when it's just me and Bop the Movie Dog sniffing the bushes and looking at the stars (he sniffs, I look), I go for maximum coatage. I don't look cool, but I feel warm.

The Lecture Circuit

FEBRUARY 16, 2007

You've got to love a university town. Last Monday a citizen with a thirst for knowledge could have attended these lectures at Penn State:

- "Spacetime Aspects of the Loop Representation of Quantum Gravity—Part 1"
- "Protein Biogenesis and Maintenance of the Endoplasmic Reticulum"
- "Non-equivalence of Delta-Separated Nets and Jacobians of Lipschitz Maps"
- "Ratoon Stunting Disease of Sugarcane"

What a lineup. An adroit lecture hopper could have gone to "Spacetime Aspects" at 2:00 P.M., gotten a taste of "Non-equivalence" at 3:30 or "Ratoon Stunting" at 3:35, and then hot-footed it over to "Protein Biogenesis" at 4:00.

Just the thought of it makes the words roll around in my head like bingo balls. "Spacetime Aspects of the Endoplasmic Reticulum!", "Non-equivalence of Quantum Gravity!", "Ratoon Stunting of Lipschitz Maps!"

Further broken down into their component words and phrases, the lecture titles sound like terrific carnival attractions, or possibly late-night, alcohol-free activities at the Hetzel Union Building. This weekend: Ratoon Stunting, Spacetime, the Loop, the Nets, and Quantum Gravity. Hold on to your hats. Wear loose-fitting clothes and rubber-soled shoes.

I didn't go to any of these lectures, but curious to find out what I missed, I made a few calls.

Visiting Professor John Baez from the University of California, Riverside, said about twenty-five people made it to his presentation, which had something to do with combining Einstein's theory of general relativity with the ideas of quantum mechanics.

I confessed that I didn't know squat about quantum mechanics.

Baez assured me that a lay person who wandered into his lecture "wouldn't have gotten more than the vaguest idea" about its content, which was geared to experts. "I made no attempt to be comprehensible to anyone but them," he said.

I was deeply intrigued by Jacobins and Lipschitz maps. I had taken a course in college on Jacobean poetry (the name of the early seventeenth-century English King James gets Latinized when used as an adjective), and my friends and I used to make prank phone calls to people named Lipschitz when we were kids.

Dmitri Burago, an assistant professor of mathematics, tried his best to enlighten me. Then he expressed concern that I would get it all wrong and make him look foolish. I told him not to worry: I was so far from even a rudimentary understanding of what he told me that I couldn't attempt to summarize it.

"Almost any mathematician with a general math background would not be lost," said Burago, whose talk drew about ten people. He imagined a physicist would probably hang in there pretty good. "Anybody else would be lost from the very beginning."

Even if they carried a Lipschitz map?

Cosima Wiese, a graduate student in the department of plant pathology, had the simplest lecture title, the easiest topic to explain to a noonoohead like me, and the most readily explainable real-world implications. Some thirty to forty people attended her talk on "Ratoon Stunting Diseases of Sugarcane."

Sugarcane diseases can cause sugar prices to rise, Weise said, "and we all consume a lot of sugar. It's pretty concrete."

She agreed that ratoon stunting, which is a thing you want not to happen to shoots growing from the root of the sugarcane plant if you grow sugarcane or buy sugar, is a funny-sounding term.

I know it sounds like I'm making news guy yahoo fun of our friends the physical scientists and mathematicians, but it's really just that I'm struck by the contrast between what I'm emphasizing in a journalism class I'm teaching at Penn State this semester and what goes on elsewhere at the university.

While the mantra in journalism is simplicity and clarity, academics often deal with unseen forces and entities and concepts that require new words if they are to be named at all. They sneer at us journalists when our quest for simplicity leads us into over-simplification, as it often does: it's not easy rendering complex situations in a few hundred words. We sneer back when they call some familiar, everyday experience by a high-falutin' name.

As a card-carrying social scientist, I'm allowed to say this: social scientists are the worst offenders. One example will suffice: I once ran across the term "human subsistence behavior" in a folklore journal. The writer was talking about eating.

Snow Bowl

NOVEMBER 7, 1997

We who were there are still thawing out.

Fans have watched football in colder weather than the thirty-four-degree conditions for the Penn State-Michigan game on November 18, 1995. But there was so much snow in Beaver Stadium that the place gave off the cold exhalations of a giant meat locker or ice chest.

First priority had been to make the field playable after a Nor'easter had dumped a foot and a half of snow on Centre County on Tuesday night and Wednesday morning. Second was clearing off the seats. That was as much as 300 volunteers and 80 state prisoners could do: the aisles remained snow-packed.

I don't care what kind of boots you have or how many pairs of socks you're wearing. Plant your feet on frozen water for three hours and the cold will communicate itself through all your layers of rubber and wool to your delicate little toesies.

Under the circumstances, many of the eighty thousand diehards at the game that came to be known as the Snow Bowl kept warm by firing snowballs at each other, at the Blue Band, and at the field. The bells of the tubas were inviting targets. So were the Michigan players.

At times, the snow throwing got so furious that from across the field, the snowballs looked like starbursts, swarms of insects, or flocks of migratory birds. The pelting got so out of control that Joe Paterno himself implored the crowd to knock it off.

The crowd complied. It was an impressive demonstration of the coach's clout.

In this snow-white world, I was the greenest of greenhorns. I had rolled into town from California a month earlier. I hadn't experienced a major snowstorm in about twenty-five years.

But everyone in Centre County was caught with their ski pants down by such a big storm so early in the season. Even the trees were surprised. They still had their leaves, which proved excellent snow collectors. Thus weighed down, branches snapped or leaned on power lines. About eighteen thousand customers lost power.

The storm, of course, proved to be only the curtain raiser on the winter of 1995–96.

A foot of snow fell from December 18 to 19. January 7 delivered seventeen inches. And so on. People couldn't rake their autumn leaves until spring. For newcomers like me, enchantment turned to amusement, then amazement.

A football weekend in State College was as much a novelty as the wintry weather: I'd never seen people with blue paw prints on their cheeks and trousers, or drivers wanting to park in my driveway, or an entire town in full party mode. I'd never heard the crowd at Beaver Stadium do the "We are/Penn State" call and response, or the PA system do the Nittany Lion snarl.

Until then, the only major college football game I'd been to was the famous fiasco in Columbia, Missouri, when officials generously gave the Colorado Buffaloes an extra down with which to defeat the Mizzou Tigers.

Michigan-Penn State was more chiller than thriller. I remember being struck by all the cool names on the Michigan squad: Mercury Hayes, Tshimanga Biakabutuka, and Amani Toomer fired the offense. Players named Irons, Steel, Swett, and Sword anchored the defense. A defensive back named Chuck Winters slipped on ice in the end zone, allowing Bobby Engram to catch a twelve-yard touchdown toss from Wally Richardson.

Then there was the play of the game, involving a holder named Joe Nastasi. Penn State faked the nineteen-yard field goal attempt by Brett Conway, and Nastasi, now a starting wideout, ran it in for the score.

"This game," cornerback Brian Miller said in the quote of the day, "was a different kind of strange."

But it didn't mean nearly as much as the one the two teams are playing tomorrow. Penn State was 6–3 in 1995; Michigan, 8–2. The teams were playing for bowl game invites, but not for a shot at the National Championship or the Rose Bowl as they are now: 1995 was Northwestern's year.

Two years is a long time in college football. And a foot and a half is a lot of snow—especially before Thanksgiving.

Hold the Foam

JUNE 14, 1998

When pundits list the technological achievements of the twentieth century, foam peanuts won't be among them.

These lighter-than-air packing materials are like bad house guests: they're a nuisance from the moment they arrive, and there's no getting rid of them.

Remember that scene in the Woody Allen movie when Woody blows cocaine off the mirror with a sneeze? Foam peanuts are like that, too, except it doesn't even take a sneeze to scatter them. Exhaling's enough.

Say a box comes to your door. If you're not too greedy, you may be able to get the flaps open without scattering the pesky pellets. But there is no way to extract the contents from the box without touching the peanuts, which flee all human contact.

So now your peanuts are on the loose, eager to explore their new home. The broom, perfect for pushing crud bombs and dust bunnies into tidy piles, is powerless against foam peanuts. Try moving a broom along the floor without disturbing the air.

Here and only here is where you should allow your children to get involved—on hands and knees, under strict supervision. Eventually the children will capture all but the bits that will turn up months later behind the drapes. Now what? If you reason that as you receive packages so shall you send packages, you will make the mistake of saving your foam peanuts instead of getting them out of the house as quickly as possible.

Of course, bringing foam peanuts outdoors is also a mistake, unless foam elephants roam your neighborhood. For the wind cannot distinguish foam peanuts from the spores and seeds that it helps propagate, and the only thing harder than sweeping up foam peanuts inside the house is sweeping up foam peanuts outside the house.

If you put the peanuts in a plastic garbage bag secured with a twisty, the twisty will loosen and the wind will find the nuts.

If you put the peanuts in a cardboard box and close the box by pulling the last flap over the first flap, the wind will find the nuts.

If you seal the box with the tape the Russians use to keep the Mir space station from coming apart, you may stop the wind from getting into the top of the box, but you will fail to stop moisture and ants from entering the bottom of the box.

I know this because last weekend I declared war on the mess in my basement. For months I had stumbled over paper shopping bags and plastic grocery bags and cardboard cartons—all leaking foam peanuts onto the basement floor. Remember that Conrad Aiken short story/"Night Gallery" episode "Silent Snow, Secret Snow?" We're talking drifts.

Thank goodness Mail Boxes Etc. functions as a foam peanuts recycling center. I did not bring them the box with the ant colony.

It would be a better world if senders of packages used Bubble Wrap, which is fun to pop, or newspapers, which are fun to read. In fact, reading the paper from Albuquerque, New Mexico, or Orange County, California, is often more fun than the gift the paper was supposed to cushion. And when you're done reading, you simply toss the paper in the recycling bin.

As for what to do with all the foam peanuts if we stop sending them to each other: let's play a joke on future generations.

New Years Day, 2101. At a ceremony, some dignitary opens our time capsule and rummages through the peanuts in search of representative artifacts of the twentieth century. And then it dawns on them: the peanuts *are* the representative artifacts of the twentieth century.

Then they all grab brooms and dustpans, and the real fun begins.

Goodbye Newsroom, Hello Classroom

AUGUST 27, 1998

The night before my first day as a professor in Penn State's College of Communications, I rehearsed various approaches to my opening remarks.

The Wiz: "I am Frank, the Great and Powerful."

The Prez: "With your help we'll build that bridge to the end of the semester."

J'accuse: "OK, which one of you stole my patio furniture?"

Yes, somebody decided Tuesday morning that they needed those tables and chairs more than we did, and though I know I shouldn't rush to judgment, especially as the teacher of a News Media Ethics course, the conclusion that this was a student job was inescapable. Still, I had to get hold of myself. The chances of the thieves being among the forty students in my Wednesday class were about one thousand to one.

Also to be settled Tuesday night was the fashion question.

I have a motto for public appearances—"Speak softly and wear a loud tie"—but the occasion of my first class entailed a footwear decision as well:

On Monday night, my four-year-old son just about kicked my big toenail off trying to dislodge a bouncy ball from between my ankles. If I had to wear sandals for the sake of my aching toe, should I go with the silver bandage that glows in holographic rainbow colors when it catches the light, or would the "Space Jam" strip make the stronger statement?

The first class, I knew, sets the tone for the whole semester, so I did not take these matters lightly.

I slept poorly Tuesday night. The fraternities down the street celebrated the eve of the new semester with—what else—a party.

Wednesday morning, I jammed my sore toe into a conventional shoe and made sure there had been no further raids on our possessions in the night.

"Knock 'em dead," my wife said as she left to teach her own journalism class at Penn State. Then I hopped on my bicycle and, eye peeled for familiar furniture, pedaled for campus. Halfway there, my bike chain fell off.

Sweaty, greasy-fingered and achy-toed, I gathered my wits and my syllabi and headed for class. I'm proud to say I made no threats, no accusations, and no promises. My fly was zipped, and there were no foreign substances between my teeth. Best of all, as far as the students were concerned, I gave no homework.

Fifty minutes of overview and I was done for the day at 10:00 A.M. Except not really.

On the face of it, a university teaching job is a pretty cush deal: a month off at the end of the year, a week off in the spring, three months off in the summer. When I tell my high school teacher friends I've got two classes this semester for a total of six hours of teaching per week, they want to beat me up.

To protect myself, I tell them that my colleagues who, like me, have moved over to the university from careers in "industry," say this is the hardest job they've ever had.

In the "real world," they worked forty, fifty, maybe even sixty hours a week but left the job at the office. Now, they prep for class, grade papers, advise students, and serve on committees by day and do the research that will advance the course of human knowledge by night.

For if they fall behind on this research, they'll be looking for work back in "the real world" faster than you can say "Promotion and Tenure Committee." Also at stake: an office with a window.

Windows display status here in the publish-or-perish sector. As junior faculty, I don't have one. Nevertheless, I was happy with my windowless office until a recently tenured neighbor in another college called the thing by its true name.

"They've got you in a closet, eh?" he said.

Another friend took pity and gave me a brass porthole. (Marine scene coming to this space soon.)

I'm not worried about earning my window through scholarly research. The hard part of the job to me is the teaching. When I started doing it part-time a few years back, a classroom veteran told me to repeat these words: "I know more than they do, I know more than they do, I know more than they do . . ."

This, I see now, was bad advice. The fact that I know more than my students impresses my students not at all. What they respect is an instructor who tells them exactly what he's going to do and exactly what they're going to do. If you're not prepared, they know it. If you're disorganized, they know that too.

Students are the real classroom veterans. Sitting there, they've got nothing better to do than evaluate your performance, and if they find that performance wanting, they'll let you know, by zoning out. It is a terrible thing to stand before a roomful of people who are zoning out.

So you have to be ready. Getting ready would be easy if it were just a matter of preparing a lecture. But lecturing has fallen into disrepute. Does this have to do with declining attention spans in the TV age? Or have Oxford students been dozing on the dons for five hundred years? All I know is, unless you're blessed with the wit of Robin Williams and the voice of Dylan Thomas, you've got about twelve minutes of yakking time before you lose them. So you have to learn how to get them talking and doing.

Still, while making my closet homey on Wednesday afternoon, I reflected on how easy I've got it compared to some of the other new hires around here. Though new on the faculty, I've been teaching part-time at Penn State for three semesters. I've lived in State College almost three years. That means I'm not settling into a new job while also settling into a new life. I don't have to unpack, open bank accounts, and learn my way around town and campus.

I just have to unbandage and rebandage my big toe. And shop for new patio furniture.

The Case of the Disappearing Porch Furniture

AUGUST 30, 1998

I let the cat out the back door the other morning and noticed that the porch looked less cluttered than usual.

Then I saw why: the patio furniture was gone—three armchairs, a lounge chair, and a round, glass-topped table.

I can't say I wasn't warned. When I bought a house amid the fraternities and student apartments in the High(rise)lands section of State College almost three years ago, a neighbor told me furniture had been stolen from my porch once before, and he advised me to lock mine up. It may be outdoor furniture to us, he said, but that's a dinette to some starving student.

If you're starving, I reasoned, you probably don't need a dinette. I decided to take my chances.

Just last week I felt fonder than ever of our lively and lovely neighborhood. Our trip to California had been nearly perfect: we loved seeing our old friends in the rural county where we used to live, and we had no regrets about having moved away.

Everyone we visited lives at the ends of long, dusty, rutted dirt and gravel roads. When I was younger, I shared this urge to live away from everyone, with wild nature as my only neighbor, where I could wander outdoors in my drawers if I felt like it.

Now I prefer the compactness and convenience and sociability of town life to the sprawl and isolation and car-dependency of country life. I'm thrilled that I can walk to work at Penn State.

The day before our furniture got swiped, I met a colleague, new to the area, who just bought a house two blocks away from us. I sang my usual praises of our embattled neighborhood. As for the students, I said, yes, they're loud and drunken at times, but they're not dangerous or destructive.

I realize now how much evidence to the contrary I chose to ignore.

Last summer, when my street was closed for repaving, I watched out the window as a guy hoisted a metal barricade with a flashing yellow light and smashed it to the ground.

Last November 1, a neighbor rang my bell at 6:00 A.M. to show me my car, which crossed the street on Halloween night and sat with rear wheels on the curb, nose in the street, and driver's door open.

In July, as we all know, drunks ran wild in Beaver Canyon.

And now we've been relieved of our ugly outdoor furniture. I can't know for certain that Penn State students are the culprits. But look at the timing: the very week the students came back to town and were looking to furnish apartments.

Last weekend, the Realtor who sold us our house stopped to chat when he saw me working in the yard. I told him, teasingly, that I would never forgive him for sticking us with a corner lot in time for the snowy winter of 1995–96.

In truth, though, one of the things I've liked best about our house is having a backyard that's open to the street and allows us to sit on our back porch and chat with neighbors out for their evening stroll.

Now there's nothing to sit on.

Every time I think of people who live in our neighborhood coming up on our porch and taking our stuff as we lay asleep in our beds, I burn with helpless rage.

Then I think of useless Bop the Movie Dog sleeping under our bed through the whole episode, and of patio furniture as the perfect cosmic symbol of suburban life, and it all just seems like another strange tale of life in the land where town meets gown.

Freeze!

Was it only a week ago that my dog and I went out for our nightly constitutional and froze in the searchlight of a police helicopter?

At first I thought it was one of those black UN helicopters, the type that would herald the coming of the New World Order.

"Steady, lad," I said to myself. "You're working too hard. The late summer heat is getting to you."

But when I blinked and shook the cobwebs out, the black bird of ill omen still hovered. This wasn't the New World Order we were seeing. This was a new weird era in the borough to be known henceforth as Police State College.

"Bop, old buddy," I said to my faithful companion, "it looks like we broke the leash law one too many times."

Instead of turning ourselves in, though, we turned tail, ducking down alleys, pressing ourselves against frat house walls, and scurrying from doorway to doorway like John Belushi in "Animal House."

"Lost them," I said, panting as the helicopter swooped toward Atherton Street. Bop panted also, but then, he's a dog.

As my heart rate slowed, I noticed our attire was all wrong. I was wearing shorts and sandals. (My legs looked ghastly in the police-state light.) Bop, I must confess, was naked.

We doubled back to the house, donned trench coats and fedoras (Bop looks great in a trench coat and a fedora) and resumed our walk. Bop, as is his custom, resumed foraging for pizza.

"Not now, you idiot," I hissed as the chopper made another pass. I spoke into my wristwatch, in French. Bop decoded the messages that had been left for him in the bushes, and encoded some messages of his own.

Risking exposure in the shelterless street, we saw that we were not the only outlaws in the Highlands. Some sat brazenly on porches or balconies. Others walked singly and in groups, as if this were legal or something.

The time, mind you, was 10:00 P.M., an hour when the law-abiding citizens of Police State College confine themselves to quarters, happy to trade their freedom for a little preventative surveillance.

Again the chopper flew over. The blades dipped so low I called out, "A little off the sides and on top, please, but leave the back long, OK?"

Perhaps, I thought, they're taking photographs of us, photos that will soon be posted on the Internet or in downtown businesses, telling us that we are unwelcome. With stakes that high, I was moved by the valor of my fellow scofflaws.

"Comrades," I cried, "I salute you. But our struggle has only begun. We must continue to walk our dogs and take our strolls every night until the forces of intimidation see that we are too many and too strong to cower in our homes, waiting for the dawn."

The dark bird flew toward University Drive.

"Ken Starr is wearing baby-doll pajamas and having phone sex with Linda Tripp," I raged against the machine. "Go spy on him. The streets are ours!"

Others picked up the chant. "The streets are ours! The streets are ours!"

We won, of course. The *CDT* reported Wednesday that the state would no longer spy on us from the air. The bird is grounded. My heart should take wing.

Alas, I miss those glorious nights. At ten o'clock, Bop hears my foot on the stair, races to the door, and bounds into the street as before. But with no searchlight and no sound of metal wings beating the air, our walks have lost their savor.

Bring back the black bird, I catch myself thinking. Then, we felt alive. Now, Bop forages for pizza, and I shuffle through the first dead leaves of the season, the old campaigner and his dog, out taking the night air.

Go! Be! Do!

OCTOBER 11, 1998

To the parents of college students everywhere I say: Back off!

In the brief time that I have been advising undergraduates at Penn State, I've seen a disturbing pattern. Under pressure from Mom and Dad, my advisees think they have to lock their wheels onto a career track and aim themselves toward a secure, well-paying job. And they don't want to yet. Or they can't decide which track to take.

One student feels like he should get an internship at a newspaper but really wants to tour with a rock band first. Another would love to live in a city and write about dance but is shying away from journalism because she fears getting stuck at a small-town paper.

I tell this one to join the band and that one to stick with the thing she loves best. They've got their entire lives to clock in, commute, make payments, and wait for vacations. What's the rush?

The rush, apparently, is to get money. The misperception is that money buys freedom. I tell my students that the people who make the most money are the ones who work the longest hours. They can't stop because they have to keep paying for all the stuff they've bought. The freest person in the world is a twenty-two-year-old with a backpack who can almost live on air and is not picky about accommodations.

This makes my upperclassmen wistful. They would love to work just to make enough money to travel, then travel until the money runs out. But it's impractical.

I disagree. Here is this vast university, offering thousands of courses on every imaginable subject. The practical undergraduate is the one who recognizes that this may be the only chance she'll have to study Chaucer, the art of ancient Egypt, the history of jazz.

The practical graduate is the one who recognizes that he can squeeze a lot of living into the gap between college and marriage, mortgage and baby carriage.

So go! Be! Do! Don't bother mapping out your life too carefully because the road always offers up detours that the map did not foretell.

Look at me, I say: BA in Creative Writing and Literature. A year unloading trucks. A year in a printing shop. Six months of youth hosteling through Europe. Grad school. Two years of museum work. More grad school. A succession of newspaper jobs. And now, a university job. I'm probably about ten years behind where I "should" be, career-wise. So what.

The hard part, I tell my charges, is figuring out what you love. Once you do, you owe it to yourself to try and see if the world will let you make a living at it. If the path dead ends, choose another one. If it goes somewhere, you may get there only to discover you'd rather be somewhere else. Interests change. That's fine. Live several lives, if you can, instead of just one.

I felt silly saying such things at first. To a forty-year-old, they're a heap of clichés. But now I'm having delusions of wisdom because I can see that to twenty-year-olds whose experience of college has consisted of deciding which conveyer belt to ride, it's news to be told that a liberal education is a valuable thing in its own right. It's news that college goes by in the blink of an eye and that it won't matter in ten years that they graduated a semester late because they changed majors. It's news that rushing headlong into a career looks silly when you consider that beyond the gold watch lies the grave.

In exchange for all this sage advice, I ask my students only one thing: don't tell your parents where you got it.

Cooties

I have the cooties. So do you. The scourge apparently has mutated—for the cootie shots we got when we were kids cannot protect us now.

I found out I had the cooties in a downtown State College bar the other night. I don't go to bars much. Happy Hour in the taverns is the nut-out hour at home—the time when a terrible confluence of hunger and fatigue turns siblings into rivals. Things calm down once we get dinner on the table, but then comes KP, lunch making, laundry folding, brushing teeth, and reading books aloud. Then, of course, we collapse in a heap.

This October, though, everything is different. The beloved Yankees of my youth are having this dream season, and I have to watch the games. Since we're terrified of the influence of television, I have to watch the games elsewhere than at home. Most nights, I've barged in on friends. But when one of the games started at 4:00 P.M., I went straight from the office to the barstool, leaving my family to fend for themselves.

So I'm sitting there on my barstool, eating entirely too many chips and pretzels, sweating out the disappearance of the Yankees' offense, when in walks my friend Steve. We shake hands, glad to see each other.

But no sooner has flesh ceased to press flesh than he whips out a bottle of antibacterial lotion, squirts a few blobs into his palm, and begins furiously rubbing his hands together like he's Lady Macbeth stained with indelible blood.

Steve quickly realizes that it looks as if he doesn't want to get my cooties and reassures me that the hand-decontamination ritual has nothing to do with me and everything to do with the platter of pot stickers that has just been set at his place at the bar. He offers me a dumpling as a peace offering, but the damage has been done. I am unclean. I am the kid on the playground from whom everyone flees. I have the cooties.

A few months ago I had a coworker at the *CDT* who kept a bottle of antibacterial lotion on a shelf with her thesaurus, her *AP Stylebook*, her *Elements of Style*, and the other tools of the newspaper trade. She had the Lady Macbeth thing going, big time.

Everywhere you look, people are arming themselves with these blue gels, and regarding each other not as friends, peers, coworkers or fellow citizens, but as carriers of contagion, as cootie garages. Every time we clasp hands to show each other "look, we come in peace," bearing no weapon, we are forced to think about where that hand has been: picking teeth, perhaps, or visiting the nose region— or worse.

We must think now of all the unclean hands that touched this dollar bill before it fell into our hands, all the grubby mitts that clenched this banister, this doorknob, this headset.

And we must think about the million mites that live in our beds, feasting on our dead skin, and the fine spray that settles on our toothbrushes when we flush an unlidded toilet, and the veritable festival of bacteria living on the sponge we use to wash our dishes or clean our kitchen counters.

In a month, the dire warnings will begin about handling raw poultry and the dangers of letting stuffing sit in the cavity of what Benjamin Franklin said should be our national bird.

Once upon a time we lived in a democracy of cooties. We passed the jug and the peace pipe. We joined hands and gave freely of our cooties and received the cooties that were freely given to us.

Now, trust no one. And keep your hands to yourself.

Images from Kosovo

APRIL 18, 1999

The photos hurt to look at: weeping women, grannies sleeping on hard ground or borne in wheelbarrows by middle-aged men, children too young to understand why they can't go home or eat more than hard bread and thin soup.

Before the photos, we said this is not our fight. These are not "American interests." Now we know that we are walking down the street and seeing an assault in progress and that we have it in our power to stop it. Do we keep walking?

So far, we've been throwing rocks from a safe distance, to little avail. We may need to get our hands bloody and to bleed.

Not our fight? That's a Balkan way of looking at it, a way that says ethnicity matters, that these people are not us. America's incomplete triumph is the doctrine that only humanity matters, that everyone is us.

President Clinton is catching flak for wanting to wage war without risking American lives. Typical boomer, he doesn't want to sacrifice; he wants it all. Can we blame him? During Vietnam, guys his age were bitter about old men sending young men off to die. Now he's the old man and he—and we—have to answer the hardest question there is: Are we willing to risk the lives of our own children in defense of Kosovars?

Before the photos, I would have said, no way. Wars are insane, a failure to control what every child must learn to control—greed, hatred, and the lust for power. Without ever having thought it through, I believed nothing was worth dying for—which is the same as saying I believed nothing at all.

Now, perhaps because it's easy to be brave when one is too old to fight and one's children are too young to fight, I'm thinking there is such a thing as a hero's death after all.

Of course, we have always known about suffering in the world and have gone about our business, plowing the field while Icarus falls out of the sky, eating ice cream while others starve, celebrating while others mourn. Callousness taints all our pleasures.

The only thing that has changed about our awareness of misery is that we now know about it specifically, immediately, and graphically. It's harder to turn away.

Yet, as my journalism ethics students point out, that's just what we did as recently as five years ago when Rwanda was dying and the West did nothing.

The harsh view is that Euro-Americans identify more strongly with the Kosovars. We see the photos and say those people look like us. We see them boarding trains and read about mass graves and torched villages and archival bonfires, and we hear the echo of the Holocaust.

A more charitable view says that we are reacting against our own failure to act during the bloodletting in Rwanda. Instead of saying, "Never again," we're saying, "Not this time."

Some of my students, in their zeal to uphold the standards of ethical journalism, berate the photographers for sticking cameras in the faces of the suffering refugees. I tell them the photos from the Balkans make me proud to be a journalist. Coming on the heels of the yearlong Bill and Monica sleazefest, and scandals involving reporters who made things up or stole voice mail or faked credentials, the images remind us that the most important thing journalists can do is bear witness to atrocity.

There can be no will to stop the ethnic cleansing in Yugoslavia unless there is an outcry against it. There can be no outcry unless the people know about it. And the people cannot know about it unless the journalists tell them and show them.

The photos of refugees are terrible and beautiful, and they are telling us that bombing may not be enough.

The Provost Was Not Amused

JUNE 13, 1999

On this high school graduation weekend, let us consider the question of commencement comportment.

At my college's ceremonies last month, the dean made the obligatory appeal for decorum during the summoning of the new Penn State graduates to the podium to receive their diplomas.

As usual, the appeal was ignored.

Once the first hoots and hollers echoed through Eisenhower Auditorium, no one wanted their grad to feel less loved than the previous grad, so the noise became competitive, as if it were being measured on an applause meter.

Some of the grads raised their arms Rocky-style to acknowledge the acclaim. Some skipped the traditional gauntlet of handshakes and exchanged high fives or hugs with their faculty guru, the dean, even with University Trustee Mimi Coppersmith Fredman.

Two graduates traded forearm bashes, as if one had just scored ahead of the other's two-run homer.

A beach ball began bouncing around the hall.

The culminating breach of decorum came when one strapping fellow surprised Provost John Brighton—Penn State's second in command—with a big, fat smooch on the cheek.

"He was not amused," reports Karen Rugh, director of university relations.

As the person in charge of planning Penn State's commencements, Rugh counts herself among those who view graduation as a solemn occasion. Others see it as a celebration where spontaneous displays of jubilation provide a welcome break from the boilerplate language of the ceremony.

One of my colleagues says if we want to put a stop to the shenanigans, the dean should warn the audience that ushers will ask them to leave if they disrupt the proceedings. Figure the odds.

Another colleague has no quarrel with the celebrating per se, but frets that cheering during one person's promenade across the stage drowns out the reading of the next person's name.

The problem, if it is one, is by no means unique to our college—or to Penn State. At the university-wide commencement last December, Penn State President Graham Spanier and speaker Jim Pawelczyk, the astronaut-professor, were frequently drowned out by the bursts of hooting and hollering.

Over the years, Karen Rugh has seen nursing students release doves indoors, forestry students wear tree branches on their mortarboards, students wear nothing under their robes, and students secrete champagne bottles under their robes—and pop the corks at the end of the ceremony.

She has not been amused.

Elsewhere, a friend tells me she heard plenty of cheering at her nephew's recent graduation from Columbia University in New York. The same thing happened at my nephew's graduation from Cornell College in Iowa.

Blame those subversive '60s. That's when students began whooping it up, pasting messages on their mortarboards, and wearing something other than formal attire under their robes, according to Penn State Harrisburg folklorist Simon Bronner. Bronner notes the trend toward puncturing "the sober tone of the event" in his book *Piled Higher and Deeper: The Folklore of Student Life.*

Generally, I could do with less hooting and hollering in the world—I hear enough from the fraternity houses down the street—and I don't like rudeness while somebody is speechifying, but I'm all for the leavening of solemn occasions.

Some say if you're going to subvert tradition, you may as well scrap the caps and gowns altogether, but it's the juxtaposition of the medieval and the modern, the robes and the Reeboks, the solemn and the celebratory that I enjoy most about graduation day.

Bronner suggests that subversion and parody are a response to the depersonalization of education at large institutions. For many of the graduates and their families, that cakewalk across the stage is their one moment in the spotlight—maybe ever.

I say let them bask in it.

Pyropetrics

This is the scariest day of the year, if you happen to be a dog. Tonight when they start the bombardment at Beaver Stadium, Bop the Movie Dog will try to dig a foxhole in our basement.

When he sees that the floor tiles will not yield to a dog's paws, he will squeeze himself down to the thickness of a loaf of bread and skitter under the lowest piece of furniture he can find.

Various members of my family may join him. We are not noise lovers, most of us, which I like to think is a sign of intelligence, though it may just mean that we are high-strung.

But at least we humans know it's only fireworks. As far as poor Bop is concerned, it's Armageddon.

The rocketry at Beaver will cap a trying week for the Bopster. First there were the steamy days. We humans complain, but we are not wearing fur coats.

Then came a series of thunderstorms, little foreshadowings of tonight's big booms. Bop dislikes thunder almost as much as he dislikes fireworks. But when rainwater began seeping under the basement door, he came out from wherever he'd been cowering to lend a hand.

Unfortunately, dogs do not have hands, so what he mainly did was get in the way. I actually yelled, "Help!" before I realized that groping through the brack-water for the drain cover at the foot of the outside steps would be a better coping strategy.

Once the drain began gulping water again, I swept puddles toward it, then shuffled around the room on an old towel to speed the drying process.

"Mooove!" I said to Bop each time he lay down in exactly the wrong spot. "Go on!" I think he was there to see that his food bowl didn't float away.

As if all this commotion wasn't enough, our cat carrier kept showing up in the front hall and in the back of the car. Don't worry, I reassured Bop. She's looking for a cat for friends, not us.

But then, while cream-cheesing a bagel, I noticed a flier in the Plexiglas recipe stand about introducing a new cat into a household that already has a cat.

Wait a minute, I said. We already have a cat, the antisocial Bimsley, who will not believe there is food in his bowl unless you go downstairs and show it to him.

Apparently the frequent visits to PAWS on behalf of our cat-less friends convinced Martha and daughters that we, too, need a new cat.

Two more, says Sylvie, the daughter responsible for bringing the guinea pigs, Bubble and Squeak, into our lives (we eventually gave them back to borough Councilman Jim Meyer and family). Two kittens.

Last Sunday, Martha tricked me into going to PAWS with her. She's been eyeballing a gray, stripy unit named Sophie and thought this might be the day to introduce Sophie to Bimsley.

I thought Sophie was scruffy-looking. I told Martha she had the same taste in cats that she had in Christmas trees. Then I realized this was also the taste she has in husbands.

I tried to make clear that I thought Bop, Bimsley, and Louis the Goldfish, not to mention three kids, were enough for one household. Martha was willing, for my sake, to consider cats other than Sophie.

The PAWS people introduced us to a big, orange guy who likes you to tickle his tummy with your toes. Martha thought he looked suspicious. I had no intention of tickling his tummy with my toes.

We did not adopt a cat that day, but Martha told the PAWS people she would be back.

When we got home I re-read the handout about introducing a new cat to your old cat. Talk about fireworks. When Bop scrunches down under the bed, I plan to scrunch down right along with him.

Year of the Ant

SEPTEMBER 5, 1999

Suddenly, the town is swarming with them.

No, no, not students.

Ants. Specifically, carpenter ants. You know, the ones that tie aprons around their thoraxes and listen to classic rock while turning wood into wheat germ.

Come on, admit it. You've got ants. It's OK. Everybody has them. It doesn't mean we're bad housekeepers.

When I say everybody, I don't just mean everybody here in State College or the Centre Region or Centre County or even Pennsylvania, though the commonwealth does have the singular honor of giving the carpenter ant its Latin name, Camponotus pennsylvanicus.

Carpenter ants are swarming into homes all over "the drought-stricken East," according to Thursday's *Wall Street Journal*. The *Journal* quotes a twenty-eight-year veteran of the ant-extermination wars who says this is the worst ant year he's ever seen.

It's certainly the worst I've ever seen. In the early part of the summer, they were congregating up where the back porch attaches itself to the house. Big blighters. They were unpleasant to look at, especially when we dined al fresco. So, like riot control cops, we began spraying them with a mixture of water and vinegar.

This had the desired immediate effect of causing them to disperse, but it did not address the underlying problem, namely, the nest. Hours later, the swarm was back.

Then they invited themselves in. I haven't seen such an invasion since cockroaches took over my apartment in San Francisco.

In those days, living alone, I treated dishwashing as a once-a-week chore, like vacuuming. The roaches loved this about me. My landlord, on the other hand, held me responsible for the entire building's bug problems. He may have been right.

I learned my lesson. Now I clean up immediately after dinner, which makes me a true grownup, but the carpenter ants swarm over the kitchen counters just the same.

Ordinarily, I am not a bug shmoosher. When I find a nasty-looking spider or millipede, my usual procedure is to trap it in a water glass, slip a piece of cardboard over the top of the glass, go outside and shake the bugger into the bushes. I don't want these freeloaders dead; I just want them gone.

But there are too many carpenter ants for such personalized service. When I see them on the kitchen counter I pound them into paste, no questions asked. This makes more of a dent in the furniture than it does in the ant population.

What we must do, I announced, is figure out how they're getting in the house. Eventually, I traced them to the doorframe leading to the back porch.

Thinking quickly, my wife patched the holes in the frame with Silly Putty. I imagined the ants taking the Silly Putty back to their nest, pressing it down over "Archie" comics and then stretching Jughead, Miss Grundy, and Mr. Weatherbee into fun-house caricatures, but in fact, the curious compound seemed to slow the ants down.

Or maybe it is just that the weather has cooled. In any case, I expect my house to fall down any minute.

If it does, it won't be the ants' fault, according to a Pest Sheet issued by Penn State entomologists. To begin with, carpenter ants don't eat wood; they just tunnel through it. Like their human hosts, they'd rather dine on sweet and fatty foods, thanks—which explains why the kitchen is such an appealing place.

It's not their tunneling that damages the wood. The wood they tunnel through and nest in is already moist and rotting. In other words, our carpenter ants may be doing us a favor by letting us know where repairs are needed.

If you drive through our neighborhood, ours will be the house wrapped in Silly Putty. Feel free to press a comic book against the siding.

Lies My Students Tell

OCTOBER 10, 1999

Here's a tip for you parents of college students: when they call you on the phone, don't believe a word they say.

This is the third semester that I have taught a class in news media ethics at Penn State. Every go-round, I have the students jot down every lie they tell for one week. The idea is to make them aware that our moral universe is a complicated place where we routinely choose between or among conflicting ethical principles.

About half of the entries in the fifty liars' journals I collect every semester are fibs told to and for friends for the purpose of preventing awkward social situations.

The other half are the whoppers they tell their parents. They want mom and dad to believe they've got their noses to the grindstone, are living clean, and are desperately strapped for cash. When in fact:

- "My mom called and asked what I did last night. I told her I did some reading and went to bed early, even though I was drinking until 4 that morning."
- "I told my mom that I attend church on a regular basis while I'm away at school."
- "I was talking to my mom on the phone and she asked me about my smoking habit. Sometimes, I'll tell the truth and admit that I'm still smoking. This time I lied and told her that I'm smoking less . . . The truth is that I'm smoking more than ever now, smoking two packs in less than three days."

- "My parents call and . . . I tack on an extra 20 bucks to the grand total of school books I purchased so that I would receive a small profit on parental reimbursement."
- "My mom called and asked . . . where my boyfriend slept and I told her he had slept on the floor, but he really slept in a bed, which also happened to be the one I was sleeping in."
- "My mom called . . . The entire conversation was one giant collection of fibs. . . . Some of the highlights include: (1) Yes, Mom, there is plenty of food in the house. (2) Yes, my classes are going to be easy. (3) How was work, it was an easy day. (4) No, I am not drinking too much, (5) Yes, I will call you tomorrow."

Scary stuff, huh?

In class, my students and I try to make distinctions between the lies they tell out of naked self-interest—to avoid blame or evade responsibility or obtain boons that they do not deserve—and "the little white lies" they tell to spare others' feelings. The ethical dilemma might be defined as honesty vs. loyalty. Loyalty usually wins.

Usually, it should. When we see an acquaintance with a new 'do, is honesty the best policy if we're thinking "Hair by Mixmaster"?

When it comes to their parental units, my students reason thus: The folks, relieved of their supervisory duties, worry about how their young scholars are managing on their own. Mom and Dad want to believe their kids are studying hard and taking care of themselves. Why tell them otherwise? What they don't know won't hurt 'em.

But are their parents that naïve? We're talking boomers here. The ones who went to college did so between the mid-sixties and mid-seventies—not exactly an age of innocence.

On the other hand, once the little birds fly away, as one of my friends' dads put it when sonny-boy went off to college, one might suspect they're flitting heedlessly about, but one would rather be spared the details.

Of course, when I ask my students to keep a liar's journal, I must also consider the possibility that they will make up their lies.

That would certainly account for this cheeky entry: "I told my dad that COMM 409 is my favorite class!"

Yup, my class.

We Need to Remember

NOVEMBER 14, 1999

At the National Civil Rights Museum in Memphis, a group of black children travels a timeline from the beginnings of slavery to the death of Martin Luther King Jr. Their guide stops often to tell the kids about this key event or that key figure. Their parents and grandparents, children of the segregated South, add their own reminiscences. And at the end of every tale of hatred and heroism comes the guide's refrain: "We need to remember that."

Civil rights activist Ken Lawrence brought the same message to the Jewish Community Center in State College last week on the sixty-first anniversary of Kristallnacht, the night the Nazis ratcheted up the terror against European Jews.

For twenty years, Lawrence, a State College resident, has been collecting postcards and letters sent to and from concentration camp inmates and showing them to students to counter those who would have us forget the Holocaust ever happened.

The Civil Rights Museum is a shrine. This is where Martin Luther King Jr. was shot and killed on April 4, 1968.

Outside, the Lorraine Motel has been restored to its mid-century motel-architecture splendor, sign and all. The turquoise doors of the first-floor rooms open onto the parking lot; its second-floor rooms open onto a covered walkway. The spot where Dr. King stood—and fell—is marked by a wreath attached to the balcony railing.

Inside, the timeline winds around the building, climbs to the second floor, and culminates in rooms 306 and 307, where Dr. King and his entourage were staying. The docent points to the open window in the brick building across the way where the shots came from. The mothers and grandmothers of the children take in the unmade beds, the newspapers, and the coffee cups, and they weep.

Before the children get away, the docent quizzes them on the museum's contents. They do well. "We need to remember," he tells them one last time.

The Civil Rights Museum shouldn't stop at King's assassination. In Jasper, Texas, thirty years after Martin Luther King's death, three white men with Nazi SS lightning bolt tattoos chained James Byrd Jr., a black man, to the back of a pickup and dragged him down the road for three miles. There wasn't much left of him when they stopped.

Students in my journalism ethics class last spring objected to newspaper coverage of Byrd's death. The stories clearly failed "the breakfast test": people who are perusing the paper while eating English muffins and Grape Nuts do not want to read graphic descriptions of a body getting torn to pieces as it bounces down a road.

Wordily, I tried to explain that there are things we may not want to know but that we need to know. In 1945, people probably would have preferred not to see the piles of bones photographed at the Nazi death camps, either. Does it nauseate you to hear the details, to see the corpses? Good. It should.

The Civil Rights Museum docent's cadences would have been more powerful: We need to remember what happened to James Byrd.

We need to know that people are still committing hate crimes in America in 1998. We need to remember that.

We need to know that people are still expressing racial hatred in 1999, here, in Happy Valley. Some idiot who calls himself "the Patriot" has been sending threatening e-mails to black students at Penn State.

The National Civil Rights Museum offers heartening evidence of a changed world. We don't see "Colored" and "White" signs with arrows pointing to separate restrooms anymore. But as I walk across campus, I mostly see white kids with white kids, black kids with black kids, and Asian kids with Asian kids.

We need to remember that the world changes, but when it comes to racial and ethnic conflict, we also need to remember that it needs to change more.

Old Eyes

About a year ago, they began printing books and newspaper with blurry type.

This was a deplorable lapse in quality control, but I tried to adjust, holding the printed matter at arm's length, then closer in, then farther out, until the words came into proper focus.

"Trombone syndrome," a friend snap-diagnosed, ignoring my complaints about declining standards in the printing industry. "You need reading glasses."

I was shocked. For years I had taken pride in my keen vision. One of the things that made meetings bearable was looking around the room and observing that I was the only one without spectacles.

I didn't need no stinking glasses. I just needed to treat a book like a bag of stinking garbage.

Months passed. Last fall, I bought a desk that came in a cardboard box: assembly required.

Assembly included fitting a Phillips screwdriver to some tiny Phillips screws. I couldn't see them. And I couldn't trombone the desk. So I called the optometrist and tried to get him to put the desk together.

No, I called the eye guy to examine my peepers. I told him about trombone syndrome, and I told him how old I was.

"Presbyopia," he snap-diagnosed. Old eyes.

Whatever shape the rest of our bodies are in, the eyes are old at forty. That's why just about every forty-year-old I know who didn't already wear glasses for near-sightedness has gotten glasses for far-sightedness in the past year. It's like losing your baby teeth in first grade.

And that is why eyeglasses showed up on the *Wall Street Journal*'s list of the top one hundred inventions of the millennium. Before specs, the *Journal* said, a craftsman would be washed up at the very age when he was becoming a master—because he couldn't see. Glasses boosted productivity, improved quality, and fostered innovation.

If glasses could do all that for me, I wanted some.

But first there was the fashion question. Since I would only wear them for reading, I was willing to get goofy glasses. But my twelve-year-old daughter, who agreed to serve as my eye-wear consultant, vetoed this idea. She thinks I look goofy enough already, apparently. Her choice: a pair of studious-looking ovals in tortoise-shell frames.

The other decision that had to be made was whether to get plain-old reading glasses, half-glasses, or bifocals. I reasoned that I was either reading or not reading. If I was reading, I would put on my glasses. When I stopped, I would take them off.

I underestimated the role of interruption in my life. I am reading—glasses on.

Someone speaks to me. I look up. The speaker is blurry—glasses off. I resume reading—glasses on. The conversation resumes—glasses off.

Inevitably, I have found it easier to slide my glasses down to the tip of my nose and peer over them, eyebrows raised. A couple of months ago, I went out to dinner with a friend I've known since we were sixteen. She, naturally, just got cheaters also. We read our menus—glasses on. Then we simultaneously lowered our glasses to the nose-tip position, arched our eyebrows, locked eyes—and cracked up. Our lost youth!

I grow old, eye grow old. I shall wear glasses at the end of my nose.

The other problem with reading glasses is that since they are not always sitting right there on my nose and around my ears where I can find them, I have to keep track of them. This is not my strong suit. In six months as a four-eyes, I've lost my glasses twice—both times, curiously, at the Nittany Lion Inn.

Even the optometrist advised getting cheapo one-magnification-fits-all glasses from a bin in a discount store and keeping a pair at home, a pair in the car, and a spare at the office.

I hope they have goofy ones.

Let There Be Laundry

JUNE 18, 2000

Pick up any poetry anthology and you'll probably find a lyric by Richard Wilbur titled, "Love Calls Us to the Things of This World."

In it, the poet's eyes open to "a cry of pulleys" and a washday miracle: the sheets, shirts, and smocks billowing from the clotheslines appear as angels in the morning light.

"Oh, let there be nothing on earth but laundry," the enraptured versifier cries.

To which I say, come over to my house, pal, and you can have all the laundry you want. In fact, you can take my place, for I am my household's "lavologist"-in-chief, in charge of washing, drying, folding, and sorting for a family of five.

Our process begins in the children's bedrooms. Unless you nag them, the children will allow their floors to disappear under a crazy carpet of dirty clothes. Nag and they'll stuff everything down the laundry chute.

When we moved into our house, we were thrilled to discover that a secret passage connected the upstairs, the kitchen, and the basement. The children couldn't squeeze their bodies down the laundry chute, but it offered perfect low-tech intercommunication among the three floors.

At less convivial moments, they would torment each other by sending a treasured possession or contested toy to the dungeon.

Best of all, they could drop a soiled garment down the chute and have it come back up folded and clean, seemingly all on its own.

Seemingly.

Generally, it is a good thing that the children throw their clothes down the laundry chute. We don't want them to wear dirty clothes. But given the high volume of laundry generated by a family of five, we also don't want to wash clean clothes. All we ask is that they give their clothes a quick once-over before banishing them to the basement.

Actually, that isn't all we ask. We also ask them to empty their pockets. To little avail. Our household launders more money than a Swiss bank. We also wash and dry candy wrappers, keys, barrettes, and, ruinously, lip balm.

These days though, fewer of our laundry problems occur in the laundry room than in the folding room, aka the master bedroom.

While countless "lavological" treatises have been written about the importance of separating the whites from the brights, of knowing when to wash in cold, warm, or hot water, of treating delicate fabrics with special care, the sorting that takes place at the other end of the process has been ignored.

Yet here I am lost. Part of the problem is the tininess of, ahem, female intimate apparel. Though the youngest female in the house is ten and the oldest is in her forties, all their undies look the same size to me. Thank goodness for my son's Teenage Mutant Ninja Turtle briefs.

Things get even more confusing when it comes to sorting pants and shorts. One might think it would be easy to tell whether I'm looking at clothes belonging to a six-year-old boy or his forty-four-year-old mother, but here's the problem:

She wears Capri pants, formerly known as clam diggers or pedal pushers. They come down to her calves.

He wears baggy "skater's" shorts. They also come down to his calves.

Am I looking at long shorts or short pants?

"Look at the waist," says the wearer of the short pants.

"Do you want to do the laundry?" I testily reply.

"Do you want me to do the laundry?" she answers.

She knows I don't, of course. I'm the one who relieved her of her post when she proved herself incapable of keeping a pair of socks together. We have, in our bedroom, an entire bin of single socks.

Materializing those missing mates would be my idea of a washday miracle.

That, and a two-way, gravity-defying laundry chute that could suck clean clothes out of the basement and spit them onto the floors of my children's rooms.

Lifeways of the Yard People

JULY 2, 2000

Before anthropology, when Europeans encountered people whose culture was drastically different from their own, they assumed such people had no culture at all.

They were wild men: savages.

Then they became primitives: they had a culture, but it was a very rudimentary culture.

Then primitives became tribal people (though not all of them organized themselves into tribes) or indigenous people (though some, like the Navajo, had migrated to their homelands from someplace else) or preliterate people (though that put them on a lower rung of the evolutionary ladder than us literate people).

Now we shy away from jamming other people into our categories. Just call them by the name they call themselves, describe their ways, or better still, let them describe their ways, and let it go at that.

So there are no savages anymore, except the ones who roam the grasslands behind the houses in my village. Formerly known as the Children, a name that defined them in terms of their relation to the dominant group, the Adults, they now go by a neutral name, the Yard people. The Adults, similarly, now call themselves the Porch people.

Some observers use words like "magic" and "innocence" and "wonder" when they describe the lifeways of the Yard people. But the Porch people find them to be nasty, brutish, and short.

The Yard people are particularly fierce before the evening meal: their ability to control their impulses declines sharply when they are tired or hungry.

At such times, they storm the porch and attempt to raid the pantry. Usually, the Porch people, with their superior might, are able to thwart these incursions and send the Yard people back outside until supper.

After some ritual complaining about how "starved" they are, the Yard people turn their ingenuity toward inventing and organizing contests.

The problem with these contests is that they require a winner and a loser, yet none of the Yard people is willing to play the loser's role.

Therefore, they cheat. They do not think of what they do as cheating. They think of it as refining the rules of the game while the game is being played. If all the players do not agree to the new rules, violence erupts.

When this happens, it is very difficult for the Porch people, as observers, not to have an impact on the observed. The Porch people believe that one should respect others and resist the urge to inflict bodily harm. They believe that these rules of conduct should apply even to one's relations with one's siblings.

"Use words," the Porch people say.

The Yard people use words. They roar and shriek them. They emphasize them with a pull of the hair, a kick, a pinch here, a punch there.

For the Yard people, fighting is part of playing. Their anger burns hot but cools fast. They do not need to apologize or forgive because they simply will forget. Their inability to hold grudges may be their most charming trait.

As for their paradoxical tendency to show the greatest cruelty to their closest companions, the Yard people understand that it is safer to release aggression with the denizens of their own yard than with strangers from other yards.

They also understand that the Porch people have enormous power over them, including the power to withhold dessert. Because they find it so difficult to think about anything other than what they want right now, they lose their dessert privileges all the time. But when dessert is what they want right now, they can be astonishingly adept imitators of Porch behavior.

"Let us be calm and rational about this," they say, though they are rarely either.

The stratagem works because it fuels the Porch people's hopes that someday the Yard people will be like them—dignified, restrained, and worthy of a seat on the porch.

Naked Run

JANUARY 7, 2001

Naked, they hurtled into the brrrave new millennium.

Unlike newborns, most of them wore hats. Seven of the eight wore shoes and socks. One made a snow angel on the homestretch.

By several important measures, the Naked Mile was a success:

- no one got arrested;
- no one got frostbite; and
- no teenagers suffered the mortal embarrassment of seeing their parents run naked through the streets of State College.

The same anarchic spirit that led a group of respectable borough residents to contemplate, then carry out, a Nude Year's sprint, almost scuttled the event. The runners argued about everything: route, attire, start time, and, above all, meaning.

The original plan, said organizers (I am withholding their names to protect their reputations), was to run a mile through the streets of State College.

The original purpose was to defy weather, age, and convention, to be symbolically reborn into the new millennium and, in the words of the Naked Mile Manifesto, "to affirm our right to be ridiculous."

But rationale became hopelessly entangled with routes and rules.

If the purpose was to shock other State College residents, nothing less than Allen Street would do.

No one had the guts to run naked on Allen Street. In fact, no one had the guts to run naked on any street with any significant pedestrian or vehicular traffic, at least not without Groucho glasses.

Groucho glasses were ruled inadmissible. So were sports bras.

Shorts and T-shirts on Allen Street found favor with the Naked Milers' teenaged children, who otherwise vowed never to speak to their parents again. But shorts and T-shirts were deemed a violation of the spirit of the Naked Mile.

Postponing until the arts festival was also deemed a violation of the spirit of the Naked Mile.

One organizer decided she was not interested in shocking anyone (translation: she was not interested in being seen by anyone) and would run in the woods or not at all. A reconnaissance team toured Lederer Park, deeming its snowy trails safe.

Lederer posed some logistical problems: Someone would have to drive, and therefore, not drink. The driver would have to be ready with blankets, cocoa, and a cover story— should a patrol car cruise the parking lot.

A supporter made a counterproposal: Exit her back yard into an alley. Dash down the alley to the street. Run one city block, then double back down the alley.

At 8:00 P.M. on New Year's Eve, a dozen celebrants gathered at the house by the alley. Until this point, no one knew how many would run. Two women had been talking it up for a year. The hosts were game. A couple showed up with bathrobes and running shoes. Another guy revealed that he, too, had brought sneakers. At 11:20, the last holdout hustled home for rubber soles.

An octet of runners solved a troubling conceptual problem. The proposed route was only a Naked Quarter-Mile. Eight people running a quarter-mile works out to a Naked Two Miles. Or does a quarter-mile, run naked in twenty-degree weather, equal one real-feel mile?

The one remaining question was whether to start at midnight or finish at midnight. (People were getting antsy.) The midnight start prevailed, but the haggling continued.

The group rejected last-minute proposals to scrap the run in favor of wheelbarrow races, three-legged races, or a conga line. A motion to run straight to District Justice Carmine Prestia's office on Fraser Street to expedite booking died for lack of a second.

And so, at the magic hour, four men and four women, all pushing or past forty-five, stripped and dashed into the snow, looking more ludicrous than lewd and lascivious—not that anyone saw them. The street was deserted.

Bells rang. Fireworks burst. Oddly, it was the warmest anyone had felt in a month of subfreezing temperatures.

"Let's do it again," somebody said.

The motion died for lack of a second.

Toss It!

FEBRUARY 18, 2001

I have given my family an ultimatum: either the Bop It goes, or I go.

If you are not familiar with Bop It, consider yourself blessed. Bop It, not to be confused with Bop the Movie Dog, is a hunk of molded plastic with a car-horn-like center and two elbow-macaroni-shaped branches extending from its center. Each branch ends in a different-colored gewgaw. To start the game, you slap the horn, which crashes like a cymbal. A rapid sequence of rhythmic commands follows, to musical accompaniment:

"Pull it!" (2, 3, 4) "Spin it!" (2, 3, 4) "Flick it!" (2, 3, 4) "Twist it!" (2, 3, 4) "Bop it!"

Those are the five possibilities, but they come up randomly. The idea is to perform the correct action—each makes its own cartoon sound-effect noise—for as long as possible. If you twist when you are supposed to spin, you're done. If you hesitate, you're lost. And if you lose quickly, the skater-dude-from-hell voice within the Bop It makes fun of you.

"Hey, you win," it says. "Not."

Or, "Nice goin'. You're out."

The device then tells you how long you lasted. It also stores the highest score. My oldest child is the household champion to date with a score of 148.

You're probably thinking I must want to get rid of the Bop It because I'm the worst in my family at it. That is only partly true. I am indeed the worse Bop It player in my family, but that may be because I have played it the least.

In fact, I hadn't played it at all until I decided to write this column. Then I needed to play for research purposes. I didn't last long.

The reason I play it the least isn't because Bop It is so hard but because it is so loud—and you can't turn it down. Can there be anything more obnoxious than a loud toy without a volume control knob?

I didn't know how good I had it when I was only complaining about the "Back Sync Boys" on the CD player and Backyard Football on the computer. Here is a sound portrait of an evening in my house before the arrival of Bop It:

"Fumble, fumble, fumble!" the glass-shattering voice of Backyard Football proclaims.

"Every little thing I do . . ." croon the boys in the band.

One daughter saws on the cello. The other tootles on the clarinet.

The UPS man rings the doorbell, and Bop, not to be confused with the game Bop It, barks furiously. Maximum and Bimsley, our dieting cats, plead for a between-feedings snack.

MBNA calls, threatening to send another new credit card.

The peppers roasting in the oven trigger the smoke alarm. The chef de cuisine turns on the exhaust fan.

The dryer buzzes in the basement. The garbage disposal pulverizes a grapefruit rind.

Only Louis the goldfish and I are silent.

You wonder how I can stand sharing my street with three fraternity houses? Now you know. I can't hear them.

The holiday rolls around. My wife hints that we should get her a Bop It for Christmas. I lower an eyebrow at her. "I think it would be fun," she says. Hmmph, I say, and buy her various noiseless presents instead.

To no avail: her evil spawn come through.

So now we have all the buzzers, beeps, bells, barks, and boy bands we had before, plus Pull it!" (2, 3, 4) "Spin it!" (2, 3, 4) "Flick it!" (2, 3, 4) "Twist it!" (2, 3, 4) "Bop it!"

I cannot be in the same room with this toy. I can't even be on the same floor of the house with it.

Neither can Louis the fish.

In fact, I declare, "Either the Bop It goes, or I go."

You wonder how my family reacted to my ultimatum?

They didn't hear me. I'm only staying because they wouldn't notice if I left.

Mob Scene

APRIL 1, 2001

Exuberance after victory we could understand. Frustration after heartbreaking defeat, maybe.

But the Penn State-Temple game was decided before the first half was half over. It got so dull we grabbed a flashlight and took turns making shadow puppets on the wall.

We watched the second half hoping only that the Lions would make a run, make it close. We cheered when they got within "a decade" of the Owls: 79–61 sounds a lot better than 81–59. The final buzzer meant we could stop watching, walk our dogs, go to bed.

Outside, we heard a sound like high wind or distant traffic or breaking waves. When you live three blocks from Beaver Canyon, you begin to recognize this sound. I got Bop the Movie Dog and walked toward the noise.

At the corner of Locust and Prospect I heard chanting: "Let him go! Let him go!" and "We are . . . Penn State!"—words that, in that context, would make a blue-and-white bleeder cringe.

Also, I heard fireworks. Bop turned tail. I dropped him off at home and headed downtown alone. I wasn't sure I was doing the right thing. I didn't want to get in the way of the police, an aggressive drunk, or a cloud of pepper spray. On the other hand, I wasn't just a rubbernecker. I was a journalist—a professional rubbernecker—and there was news happening down the street.

I found a spot on the lawn of Grace Lutheran Church where I hoped I could observe the mob without joining it. The police were trying to keep Beaver Avenue open to traffic. Bottles crashed. People dashed into the streets and pounded on the hoods of crawling cars.

One guy charged into the middle of the intersection, dropped his drawers, and waggled his rear.

Out came the pepper spray. Three guys stumbled toward me, weeping and rubbing their eyes, collapsing on the grass behind the Grace Lutheran sign. A girl riding piggyback begged for water.

The crowd split, some fleeing down Garner Street, some loping east on Beaver. As the mob thinned, it got quieter. Since it didn't look like there would be any overturned cars or toppled streetlights or burning sofas, I decided I had seen what there was to see and headed home.

Now I'm trying to makes sense of what I saw.

To some extent, the disturbance—let's not call it a riot—was an accident of scheduling. Probably 10:00 P.M. Friday was not the time the borough police would have chosen for the opening tip-off. Whatever the outcome of the game, there were going to be a lot of liquored-up fans pouring into the streets after midnight.

We know that drunks are loud. We know that noise draws crowds. The mob sucks people into itself. The bigger and louder it gets, the more people want to see what's going on. Most of the people I saw on Beaver Avenue had more in common with me than with the guys who started to rock the streetlights: they were lookie-loos, not hooligans. Too many of them, from what I hear, got face-fulls of pepper spray.

Still, this latest Beaver Canyon mob scene was the most disturbing one yet. The first two could be understood as the excesses of a midsummer festival. The gathering after the North Carolina game could be seen as a spontaneous celebration of an upset victory.

But the raucous reaction to the blowout loss to Temple seemed more ritualistic than spontaneous. It said: This is what we do here. This is part of the culture of this place.

Expect more. Expect worse.

When It Rains, It Floods

JUNE 24, 2001

There is a grandeur, a majesty about cascading water that you cannot fully appreciate when it comes to rest in the basement of your house.

At first we blamed the little drain at the foot of the outside steps that lead to the laundry room door.

During gully washers, when water would pour off the roof in sheets, backyard dirt would wash down the steps and clog the drain. Water would rise to the level of the doorway, and in it would come.

In five years, we had had one major flood (water beyond the laundry room), a couple of minor floods (laundry room only) and several near-floods. Solution: be diligent about sweeping the steps and clearing the drain.

When that didn't work, we concluded that the drain was too small for the job it needed to do. My wife, who is home more often than I, developed a set of flood emergency procedures that mostly consisted of laying towels across the doorways of the other rooms of the basement. The idea was to confine the waters to the laundry room and the hall.

Eventually (we are rather slow-witted when it comes to household repair and maintenance) it occurred to us that it is not normal for water to pour off the roof in sheets. It is supposed to run into gutters, which are supposed to channel it down spouts, which are supposed to carry it away from the house. This was not happening.

So we called the gutter guy. The gutter, he noticed, had pulled away from the house directly above the basement steps. Unchallenged, the water was behaving like river water where the riverbed declines. It other words, it was falling.

The gutter guy closed the gap. That was last summer. Now downpour season has come around again and we find that the stairwell is filling with rainwater again. This time, I think, it really must be a clogged drain. I had grown lax about the bits of leaf and bloom and seed casing that collect on the stairs. So with heavy rains predicted for Saturday, I sweep the steps and snake the drain.

Then the deluge begins and pours off the roof in sheets. Our gap is back.

The drain needs my help. I begin bailing.

Then I need my wife's help. We develop a system. I scoop pails of water out of the stairwell and dump them into larger buckets stationed at the laundry room door. Martha empties the buckets into the laundry room sink.

We can't keep up. The water laps into the laundry room. I rip the lids off the trash barrels and place the barrels under the waterfall. The kids position beach buckets and yogurt containers on the stairs.

The rain keeps coming. The trash cans fill. I empty them on the lawn. The water spreads from the laundry room to the hall.

Upstairs, I hear music. I feel like I am in the bowels of the Titanic while passengers in tuxes and evening gowns twirl across the dance floor overhead.

One of my children, the one to whom everything happens, comes down the steps to see how we are doing—and slips on the wet tile floor. She complains of elbow pain. Martha takes her to the emergency room. I keep bailing.

Finally, the rain lets up and I move into the mop-up stage. The fatter of our two fat cats appears and can't understand where his food bowl is and why I am not dropping everything to find it and fill it. The dog shows up and makes himself at home. The basement smells exactly like him.

Martha calls.

The bone is bruised, not broken.

I scan the sky for a white dove with a sprig of laurel in its mouth. Seeing none, I call the gutter guy.

Don't Expect to Be Bored

Welcome back, scholars. Ready to work? Of course you are. You want to enjoy this class, don't you?

You're smirking. What does enjoyment have to do with school, or work?

The answer, my friends, is: everything.

I know: spoken like a geeky professor.

You equate enjoyment with leisure, with playtime, with entertainment. I'm here to tell you that one of the best feelings in the world is pride in a job well done.

I know: what a corny phrase.

Think of what you enjoy most. (For the purposes of this discussion, we'll limit ourselves to the most fun you can have with your clothes on.)

A concert by your favorite band? Watching a football game with friends? A day at the beach or the amusement park? A night on the town or at a party?

The beauty of these experiences is that they take us out of ourselves: we appreciate the grandeur of someone else's achievements or of nature. Or we revel in sheer physicality: the rush of the roller coaster, the texture of wet sand, the rhythm of the dance.

Maybe your idea of a good time is going all out on the basketball court or on a bicycle or on skis. Instead of letting go, you're grabbing hold, concentrating, persevering. It feels good to do, and it feels good to have done. Brainwork is the same.

According to psychologist Mihaly Csikszentmihalyi—don't worry, his name won't be on the test—"the best moments of our lives occur when a person's body or mind is stretched to its limits in a voluntary effort to accomplish something difficult."

So I'm asking you to work. That includes in the classroom.

Don't come in here thinking you're an audience member—because I don't intend to put on a show.

Don't think learning has nothing to do with what you do and everything to do with what I do. All I can do is help you teach yourself.

Look, I have been at this long enough to know better than to expect to walk into a roomful of passionate scholars, or to flatter myself that I can transform you into passionate scholars by the sheer force of my charisma and erudition.

A lot of you are here to pick up your ticket to the workforce. So be it. You should work hard anyway—not for my sake, but for yours. The alternative is boredom.

A couple of semesters ago, one of my students attended a speech and began her reaction paper by admitting that she had "expected to be bored." I realized a lot of students enter the classroom with the same expectation. If you approach experiences expecting to be bored by them, I scribbled furiously in the margin of her paper, more often than not, you will be.

"Ever to confess you're bored," wrote the poet John Berryman, "means you have no inner resources." Berryman went on to conclude that he had no inner resources. Then he went on to kill himself.

You don't have to worry about my boring you to death in this class because only you can bore you. It's a choice, an attitude, a failure to take an interest, a self-fulfilling prophecy. Worst of all, it's a habit of a lazy mind.

I am asking you to break the boredom habit this semester. Try walking in the door with the intention of getting as much as you can out of these seventy-five minutes. Try behaving as if you, too, are responsible for what goes on in this room.

Can't wait to get started, can you? Good. On Thursday we'll discuss the first fifty chapters of our book.

Have fun.

Back to School and Out the Door

SEPTEMBER 2, 2001

It's going to be an interesting week at my house. This is the week our oldest child starts high school.

The middle child starts—you guessed it—middle school.

This is the week our youngest child must make his way to elementary school unescorted by a big sister.

Three kids—three schools.

This week, my wife and I will wish we had our own bathroom, for this was the summer our youngest child made the transition from evening baths to morning showers.

Five people—one shower.

This week, our children, who had been going to bed at midnight all summer, will have to throw off their blankets at 6:30 A.M.

Call us irresponsible parents, but I blame those night-owl Europeans we visited in June and July. If you've ever eaten dinner in Europe, you know that nobody sits down to eat before 9:00 P.M. and that it is not unusual to remain at the table for three hours.

On one memorable evening, we ate the last bites of a blue, glow-in-the-dark dessert called a policeman's hat at 1:00 A.M. Needless to say, late-night dining did not lend itself to early morning sightseeing.

We are going to have to ask our neighbors, the frat boys, to be particularly considerate this week.

Last week, I must confess, I called the cops on Monday morning, complaining of loud music. This is my policy: they can go crazy on the weekend, but weekday nights they have to be considerate of those of us who have to chase our kids out of the shower in the morning.

"I hate to bust these guys on their first weekend back," I told the dispatcher, "but it's 1:40 A.M. and I can't sleep."

"They're here for an education, sir," the officer responded. "We'll be right over."

If you're scoring, that was my third call in nearly six years.

We are going to be particularly interested this week in monitoring the child who has had her light bulbs confiscated on more than one occasion to prevent her from reading until dawn, then sleeping until noon.

In years past, she barely made it out the door at 8:30 A.M. Starting this week, she's going to have to be ready an hour earlier.

Oh, there is going to be weeping and wailing and gnashing of teeth at our house this week.

My daughter, Rosa, curiously, thinks I can't wait. For my birthday last week, she drew me a comic strip.

First panel: Despite the fact that there is a birthday cake on the table, a round-faced, bewhiskered, curly-haired guy who looks suspiciously like the mug shot that accompanies this column is trying to read a newspaper called "The Dull Times." The headline on the lead story blares, "Man Drinks Water."

Second panel: Dad has put down his newspaper. The headline now reads, "Squirrel Dies." The children are squabbling.

Ethan: "Can we eat now?"

Sylvie: "Rosa's chewing loudly. Ethan's eating frosting."

Rosa: "Sylvie's being mean."

Third panel: Dad is fleeing, necktie flying. "Aaaaaah!" he shrieks. The children call after him, "Dad!"

Fourth panel: Dad has returned and is about to open a package. The caption says, "The best birthday gift." The legend on the box reads, "Back to School."

I suppose Rosa is right. If we can get her and her siblings out the door and back to school, life will be grand.

But that's a big if.

Not Quite Business as Usual

SEPTEMBER 16, 2001

Cancel, or carry on?

That's the question everyone had to grapple with on Tuesday.

On campus, we got word from Old Main that instructors were "free to exercise their judgment about holding or canceling classes."

With an hour to go before my journalism ethics class, I walked over to the HUB to watch the news on the big television.

The place was packed. Looking around, I wondered if these kids were going to be drafted to fight, but then wondered if that kind of massive deployment of troops had any relevance to this new kind of war.

At 12:30 P.M., still trying to decide what to do about my class, I spotted my friend Dan Walden. Dan retired three years ago after a thirty-year career at Penn State, but he can't seem to stay out of the classroom: he continues to teach one course each fall, for no pay.

Under the circumstances, I felt like a stumblebum fairy-tale hero who had found his magic helper.

Dan, I said, I have class in half an hour. Advise me.

True to form, the emeritus professor answered my question with a question:

What do terrorists want? To disrupt our lives. Don't let them. Teach your class.

The next question was, how? Business as usual or a discussion of the day's events? Gauge the mood, Dan said.

So I did. No one wanted to talk about the scheduled topic. In that sense, we did let the attacks on New York and Washington disrupt our lives. At the same time, a discussion of the unfolding coverage of a major news story perfectly fit the theme of the course, to say nothing of the mood of the class.

Mostly we talked about the pitfalls of nonstop network news. The poor anchors have to keep talking. In the early going, especially when little is known and everyone is watching, they repeat, ad nauseam, what they have already told us. The pressure, at those moments, to tell us something new is tremendous.

Beware of speculating experts, I told my class. Appreciate the role of the journalists.

Carry on.

That afternoon, several of my colleagues and I gathered outside our offices for an impromptu discussion of what and how to teach on such a day. We knew we weren't all-knowing and all-wise. We were just grownups, maybe the only grownups available for some of our students. We could let them come to grips with the day's events on their own, or we could attempt to provide a bit of perspective.

We owed it to them to try.

Twenty-four hours later, it was time to "gauge the mood" of my freshman seminar. What had been their experience that morning and the previous afternoon? Did they want to talk, or were they sick of talking?

Most of their classes had either been cancelled or business as usual. They resented business as usual. They wanted to talk.

Here, too, the theme of the class fit the situation at hand. The class is about storytelling. The need to make sense of a senseless experience and connect with other people by sharing stories is never greater than after a cataclysm.

The students struggled to articulate the sense of reality and unreality that comes from watching events on television. Many of them had friends and relatives in New York and Washington. That made it real. But there they had been on a gorgeous day in Happy Valley. That made it unreal.

Were their lives about to change? How? And for how long?

The lead photo in Tuesday's *New York Times* showed "designer graffiti" over the entrance to New York Fashion Week tents. How long until we see a fashion photo on the front page of the *Times* again? When will it no longer sound absurd to say, "Quiz Thursday"?

Who knows? In the meantime, we carry on.

Nothing But a Pack of Cards

SEPTEMBER 23, 2001

Sometimes I imagine a cartoon truck bearing down on me, malice in its headlight eyes.

I know I can't get out of the way. I know I'm done for. I have just enough time to think, man, if I knew this was going to happen, I sure wouldn't have spent my last hours on earth grading papers.

Those jets slicing into the World Trade Center like knives into melons remind us of what we always know and try to forget: any hour could be our last.

Why, then, do we fritter away our lives in foolish pursuits? What should we do instead?

Now my office door opens onto the streets of lower Manhattan. I see my little drifts of books and documents for what they really are: trash.

And I can understand, now, how some people wake up in the morning and can't think of enough good reasons to get out of bed.

Life fell apart on September 11. Now we have to put it back together.

Economic necessity would be one good reason to get out of bed. It costs money to lounge around. It costs money to eat. The culture has constructed this fantastically elaborate system of work-for-pay. Participate, and you can leave the big questions to the philosophers. Tell yourself that being rewarded for your work must mean that the work is meaningful. Tell yourself that you are contributing in some small way to the maintenance of the social order.

Oh, it's a game, to be sure: Let's pretend all this matters. I'll be the professor, you be the students. OK?

You turn in an assignment a day late. Lose one letter grade.

My article gets mixed reviews from a prestigious academic journal. Go back. Revise and resubmit.

You pass the class! You graduate! Here's your piece of paper. The editor has accepted my article! I get tenure! Here's my piece of paper.

As the game wears on, the paper piles up. Some of it we trade for material goods. It's fun, at times, hopping around the board, performing the required tasks, getting and spending. It feels, at times, like we are actually getting somewhere.

But the game is flawed. No one can win. The only way to end it is to tip the board over and scatter the playing pieces. Leave it to Lewis Carroll's Alice to utter the unutterable:

"You're nothing but a pack of cards."

And, "I don't believe there's an atom of meaning in it."

So then what? Switch games? Hedgehog croquet, anyone?

Whatever, right? The point is, we must act. Boredom is the other reason to get out of bed in the morning. Mind and body demand their stimulation. There may be a message there: The imperative to act makes action meaningful. We discover what we can do that brings us pleasure, what we can do that's useful. Thus do we fill our days and construct our lives.

We also discover that the actions of others can be pleasurable and useful. And that leads to the most important discovery of all: we, too, can bring pleasure and do useful things for others.

Since September 11, people have wanted to know what they could do to help. Perhaps the answer for most of us, after we have given blood and donated cash, is the simplest one, the one that sounds almost inane in the telling: Help people believe that their lives matter. Be kind. Bring joy.

All of us suffer from crises of meaning. Compassion and joy make it better. They don't just compensate us for the lack of meaning. They make meaning. Our lives matter to the extent that we treat each other as if our lives mattered.

Care and delight and know that you will be missed when the knife slices through air and the truck bears down. Then you can get back to those piles of paper.

The Solace of Routines

SEPTEMBER 30, 2001

As I opened the front door to get the paper the other morning, I wondered how the Yankees had done the night before. (They lost but clinched the division anyway because, true to form, the Red Sox lost.)

And just like that, I realized that the attacks on the Pentagon and the World Trade Center had slipped from foreground to background.

Every precious day since September 11, I had gone downstairs and tried to scan the front page, listen to the radio, and make coffee all at the same time, as thirsty for my morning update as I was for my morning brew.

The attacks shattered us in some way, but they did not shatter our routines, at least not for long. They couldn't. As long as there were jobs to go to and lunches to make and lessons to drive the children to, we had to do what we always do, even if what we always do now seemed like a set of rituals that we no longer understood.

From April to October, my routine includes following the Yankees. Of course, it's absurd to care about the Yankees at a time like this but let's face it: it's absurd to care about the Yankees any time (a point anyone from Boston would readily concede).

What's different is that now it feels insensitive: Oh sure, easy for me to move on. I didn't lose anybody. I don't live in New York anymore.

A few days ago, I heard, secondhand, about a State High grad who came home from New York University the weekend after the attacks, seeking solace from friends and family.

She didn't find it. Despite our flags and our tears, it hadn't hit most of us, two hundred miles away, the way it had hit her, at

"Ground Zero." She had to evacuate her dorm. She smelled the smoke and breathed the dust. We watched it on television.

As close as television brings the world, it also flattens and shrinks it.

"You don't even begin to get it, to get what it was like looking up at that," folksong writer Jack Hardy told the *New York Times*. "I saw that building go down knowing my brother was in it. Coming down, slowly and surely crumbling. It made me angry at every disaster film ever made, because they don't begin to have the horror. I headed down the West Side Highway until I was knee-deep in ash."

Another story in the *Times* talked about people who made their way downtown to gape and take pictures. Some of the terror-tourists admitted to feeling ashamed of themselves but said they simply had to see it "with their own eyes." The sense I had is that they were there because they wanted to feel it more deeply, that television hadn't made them feel it deeply enough.

I've seen countless stories counseling parents about what to tell their children and how to calm their fears and respond to their nightmares. In New York, these stories might make sense, but for my own children, the attacks have been background from the first. They understand that this terrible thing has happened and that neither the adults on the radio nor the adults in the master bedroom can stop jabbering about it. But the sun rises and sets, their teachers assign homework, and their soccer coaches expect them to show up and play the games—just as Joe Torre expects Roger Clemens to show up and play the games.

So we all show up and do our bit. There's something monstrous about resuming normal behavior amid the grief and the rubble and the possibility of worse to come, but there's also something heroic about it.

"I can't go on," the playwright Samuel Beckett wrote. "I'll go on."

Of course we do. After all, as my dad would say, consider the alternative.

Little Idiot Children

My parents did a crazy thing in October 1941. They got married.

Europe had been at war for two years. German U-boats were sinking American ships. European Jews were being deported to Polish ghettos, forced to wear the Star of David, massacred in Poland and Russia and France.

Surely my parents knew it was only a matter of time before America got sucked into the vortex. Surely these first-generation American Jews had at least an inkling that Hitler meant what he said about the final solution to "the Jewish question."

Think how brave they were to get married at such a time. This was more than an act of love. It was an act of defiance and of affirmation.

To get married is to believe in the future. It's to look beyond being lovers, beyond the passion of right now, to "making a life together," to the companionship and comfort of the long haul.

That couldn't have been easy in 1941.

"Whaddaya talkin' about?" my dad says in his best Bronx brogue. "If anything, people were feeling optimistic. We were coming out of the Depression years. We thought we were safe as long as we minded our own business."

My mother agrees: "We were happy-go-lucky and we felt we had our future ahead of us. I think we were like little idiot children."

Children, they were. He was twenty-three, she, nineteen. During the wedding ceremony, my dad was so nervous he chewed gum. They spent their honeymoon in their new apartment in Brooklyn. At first, the only furniture was the bed. They ate their meals on the windowsill. They spent their days tooling around in a 1935 Ford, "a rickety, cockamamie little car," buying furnishings for their new home.

Two months later, the Japanese attacked Pearl Harbor.

"Of course," my dad says, "that's when our world changed."

To stay on the home front with his bride, my father traded his printer's apron for a job in an aeronautical plant in Philadelphia: workers in essential industries would get called up last. That bought him and my mother a year together. Basic training in Miami Beach, followed by stops in Los Angeles, and Greenville, South Carolina, bought them another year. Finally, my father shipped out for England, made it home safe, and resumed married life.

If the war had started any sooner, my dad says, there would have been no wedding. Who would want to risk leaving a grieving widow?

But could they really not see the war coming? The Holocaust?

"The country got caught with its pants down," my father says of Pearl Harbor.

My parents heard vague reports that "Jews were disappearing." My mother recalls her parents getting "disturbing" mail from relatives on "the other side."

"But there must have been guilt on the part of those who couldn't do anything," she says, "and about having left family behind in the first place. They didn't discuss it."

"Nobody could guess at the enormity of what was to follow," my father says.

I think my parents' story tells us a lot about ourselves as Americans. We live in a fool's paradise. In 1941, we believed that the rest of the world was very far away and that our country was protected by its oceanic moats. Sixty years later, we still believed it. Judging from how we reacted to Pearl Harbor and the Cuban Missile Crisis and the 1993 bombing of the World Trade Center, we'll probably resume believing it.

We're "little idiot children," as my mother puts it. But we're also the most optimistic people who ever lived. Indeed, if optimism is a self-fulfilling force, it may be the secret of our success.

Look at my parents. They may have been crazy to believe in a bright future in 1941, but here they are, sixty years later.

The endurance of any good thing—art, friendship, marriage—gives us all hope.

Under a Dark Sky

I found the book I was looking for at the far west end of level 2A in the Pattee Library stacks. Then I sat down at the last desk in the long row of desks along the windows over Curtin Road.

I got out my notebook, put on my glasses, and was about to start reading when I noticed a piece of clear tape stuck to the desk with a word scribbled on it in blue ink. The word was "anthrax."

My first thought was to move to another desk: maybe an anthrax spore was under the tape.

Nah. The only explanation for the presence of this word on a desk in a far corner of a university library in central Pennsylvania is that whoever wrote it is obsessed. We're all obsessed.

Anthrax is everywhere. Bombs are everywhere. I was sitting on my porch late one recent afternoon when I heard, and then saw, an airliner flying low over State College. We don't get them that big at University Park. They don't normally fly that low over this area. In a few hours, it would be time for Monday Night Football in the Meadowlands. I became convinced this was another hijack attack.

A few days later, I read about mounting tensions between India and Pakistan, terrorist training camps in the Philippines, terrorist threats against American interests in Indonesia and Malaysia. I became convinced we were witnessing the start of World War III.

I don't want you to think I'm hysterical or that I spend my days trying to decipher coded messages in tapes of Osama bin Laden. I do my work. I watch the leaves dance down from the maples on my street. I watch the baseball playoffs on TV. I sleep.

But it's always there: not fear, exactly, but an edgy awareness that at any moment while I'm working or enjoying the pleasures of the season, there could come the summons to the radio or television: They've bombed the Empire State Building. They've blown up the George Washington Bridge.

There's a television in the lobby of the building where I work. It's always on and it's always tuned to CNN. I used to ignore it. Now I go out there every hour or so. If a commercial's on, I go back to my office. If I see the "Breaking News" banner, I stay to find out what's happening.

This is what people mean when they say nothing will ever be the same, that no one will ever feel safe. Wars have always ended with the defeat of armies, the conquest of land, the losers' recognition that they don't have the resources to win. But this feels like it can end only when the sense of grievance ends. And we look at the Middle East and Northern Ireland and the Balkans and elsewhere, and we see that the grievances never end. Killing bin Laden won't do it, not as long as the children of bin Laden are raised in a culture of terrorism.

At best, we can hope for the terror to subside—either because it really does take a charismatic figure to mobilize the anger, or because this war is going to reconfigure the relationship between the Islamic world and the West in ways we cannot foresee.

In the meantime, we are living under a dark sky. We listen. Nothing. We watch. Nothing.

We almost want the heavens to open up just to break the tension, to dispel this crackling, heavy air. Almost.

In France some years ago, I joined the Parisians dancing in the street on Bastille Day, thrilled to see this after-image of the public joy that greets the return of peace after a time of war. I wonder if we will experience such a moment here. And when.

Let Us Commence

MAY 12, 2002

Any year now, I am going to become so august a personage that universities will vie for my services as commencement speaker. To prepare for that eventuality, I have written a practice address to the class of 2002.

Welcome to the world of grown-ups. Here is some advice for making your way in it:

- Do good work. (I stole this one from Garrison Keillor.) You can probably get by if you just do the minimum, but unless you're extraordinarily lucky, don't expect to gain much money, recognition, or satisfaction.

   In a culture dominated by the promotion of entertainment and fun, work gets equated with drudgery, with doing what you need to do to get money so you can do the things you want to do. In fact, doing good work—which is to say, skillfully doing work that is worth doing—makes us feel better about ourselves than almost anything else we do.

   Look at it this way: For the next fifty years you're going to spend about a quarter of your time working. Would you rather endure it or enjoy it?

   One other thing: "My alarm didn't go off" is not going to cut it with your future employers. Bosses are more like elementary school teachers than college professors when it comes to attendance and tardiness. They expect you to show up—on time—even on the days immediately preceding or following your vacation. It has to do with paying you money.

- Think of yourself as a member of a community. Participate in local politics, at least as a voter, even if you're just passing through. In a mobile society, we have to rely on each other to make intelligent decisions about local issues. Try to learn more about your neighbors than you know about Hollywood celebrities and sports stars.
- Be considerate: Your actions affect other people. Don't pretend you don't see someone you know. Don't ignore a mess just because you didn't make it.
- Be a "mensch," which is Yiddish for a person who is patient, honorable, and kind. Remember that the people you care about need reassurance that you care about them.
- Be flexible. Things do not always go as planned. Understand that there's no perfect job, no perfect place to live, and no perfect mate. Before you complain, think about how little you have to complain about. Don't blame your troubles on other people.
- Don't spend too much time talking on cell phones, listening to portable CD players, or looking at screens. In connecting us at a distance, these devices disconnect us from the world around us. Dare to be alone with your thoughts. Limit your exposure to commercial messages, which seduce us into equating happiness with consumption.
- Slow down. Speeders tend to be less courteous to pedestrians and to fellow drivers, and more likely to do grave harm to themselves and others. Give yourself enough time to get places, and you will live a calmer life.

If none of this sounds as fun as partying, keep in mind that your idea of fun changes as you get older. Or do any of you still play with blocks?

In fact, your idea of fun may change so much that fun will cease to be the right word for it. Fun is fast and loud and maybe a little scary, like an amusement park ride. Adults care more about pleasure, joy, appreciation, satisfaction.

Remember that we call this commencement: The best part of your life isn't over. It's just beginning.

No Magic Circles

Call off the search for the meaning of life, the secret of happiness, and the key to success.

It's not wearing sunscreen or doing the hokey-pokey or loving thy neighbor or smelling the roses or performing random acts of kindness.

It's—wait, I have it here somewhere—oh, yeah: it's getting organized.

I didn't have to climb any mountains or ford any streams to learn this great truth. I just had to go to back-to-school night.

In America's public schools these days, getting organized is job one. In fact, it may be the only job. As I went through the hurry-up version of my daughter's day (seven periods in sixty-three minutes), I waited for her teachers to tell us what, exactly, our young scholars would learn once they got organized.

It was like watching someone endlessly shuffle a deck of cards. I wanted to yell "Deal!," but there was only more shuffling.

As far as I can tell, students aren't learning how to be organized as a prelude to performing particular tasks. They are just organizing for organization's sake. As often happens—think of the desire to amass great wealth—the means have gotten confused with the ends.

I suspect the rage for organization is a reaction to the decades of disorganization that followed the 1960s. Back when the cool teachers were draft dodgers who circled the desks and compared John Donne's "No man is an island" to Paul Simon's "I Am a Rock," we didn't busy ourselves with copying our assignments into our assignment books. The public school's mission, as those guys saw it, was to mold the anti-organization man and woman, to save us and the world from the war machine.

I knew the '60s were over when a classmate in the first college class I ever took proposed arranging the chairs in a circle and the professor growled, "There are no magic circles."

Now there are only magic folders and magic test scores. Parents demand accountability. We get accounting. Teachers devise procedures to ensure that paperwork and assignments get completed, signed, and turned in on time. They spend more time thinking about class management than they do about teaching.

Now it is unpatriotic to question the wisdom of waging war on Iraq.

And so the pendulum has swung. That's what pendulums do. Even I, a disorganized child of the '60s, have developed a keen appreciation for the need for organization. In fact, I'm sure the only reason I'm not rich and famous is that I'm not organized.

I'm equally sure that the only reason my life hasn't collapsed around my ears is that I have a good memory. I don't put anything anywhere that makes any sense, but I retain a mental picture of where I put it that enables me to find it—eventually. Once the Kubek-Richardson-Mantle-Maris cells go, I'm doomed.

Messing around with color-coded binders and dividers therefore makes perfect sense to me. My only problem with "get organized" as the answer to life's burning questions is that it's rather a boring answer. It turns us into paper-shuffling Prufrocks who measure out our lives in planners and Post-it notes.

As a journalism instructor, I can't say I'd mind getting students who were taught that rigor is as important as self-expression. As a parent, though, I'd like to know what else my children will learn once they master the art of keeping their math homework from disappearing into their science folder.

Ship of Fuels

OCTOBER 13, 2002

The places are set. The diners are seated. Dinner is served. The host picks up her fork. The meal begins.

One of the diners is not really seated after all. He hovers above his plate like it's a flower and he's a hummingbird.

Ordered to put his bottom on the chair, he sits and kicks the base of the table over and over, as if it were a bass drum pedal.

Ordered to cease and desist, he tells the entire plot of a TV show that no one is sorry to have missed.

He is not eating his dinner.

Queried, he announces that he hates his dinner. The host tells him he is welcome to take over the cooking duties. He's thinking of M&Ms.

Meanwhile, one of his dining companions painstakingly separates her meal into its constituent parts. Queried, she declares, with passion, that she hates cooked tomatoes. She, too, is invited to assume the cooking responsibilities. She, too, has lots to say. Much of it entails correcting the myriad errors in the narratives of the first diner.

The third diner is stunned into silence. She cannot believe she is dining with such losers. Fortunately for her, the telephone rings near the end of the meal, so she can slip away from the table and not return. Somehow the other two slip away as well, leaving me and my wife to clean up and wonder why we bother trying to maintain the family dinner tradition.

Back in the days of bibs and booster seats and sippy cups, the house was like a cruise ship. No one could go anywhere, so everyone could be expected to show up for the six o'clock seating. Indeed, some nights were like adventures on the high seas, with food and drink spattering the floor and walls.

Now the waters are calmer, but with soccer and swimming and boyfriends and Girl Scouts, there are only three nights a week when all the passengers remain on board. Should we give in and become one of those families whose members forage for their own food and eat standing up or in the car or straight out of the pot or while doing homework on the dining room table?

The children wouldn't mind. To them, eating is a natural activity: when the furnace needs fuel, you stoke it.

To us, though, eating is cultural, which is to say, communal and ritualized. We want everyone to sit down at more or less the same time, each in his or her accustomed place around the table, napkins in laps, forks left, knives right, and to bask in each other's company and keep each other abreast of interesting developments in their lives.

Sometimes, it is true, we resort to going around the room and asking everyone to recount the highlight of their day. Sometimes, depressingly, no one can think of a highlight. But we cling to the idea that a family is not a bunch of strangers on a ship, thrown together by chance. The busier everyone is, the more important it is to take a half-hour out of the day to sit down together.

Even if the conversation consists of interminable, pointless, unfunny stories.

Even if the conversation consists of interminable arguments between people who don't know what they're talking about.

Even if one diner in particular sings, interrupts, fidgets, thumps, makes gross sounds, or speaks of gross things.

Even if no one says anything at all.

Even if everyone complains about the food?

Let them eat M&Ms, just as long as everyone eats them together.

Questioning Authority

My son is doing research on the nature of power and authority.

He is not going to the library or the web for this information. He is doing fieldwork. His house is the field. We, his parents, are the human subjects.

His method is elegant. He defies all our commands and takes note of what happens.

He observes that we become angry. Continued defiance enables him to catalog the various forms our anger takes: We raise our voices. We banish him from the dinner table or send him to his room. We withhold various privileges: dessert, movies, music, playing with friends.

He notes that we do not beat him (though we are sorely tempted), that we grant pardons, that even when he runs out of chances, the punishments are not that bad: his room is not without comforts and diversions and, in any event, he seems willing for now to make a few sacrifices in the pursuit of his research agenda.

In short, at age eight he is learning that our power over him is largely contingent on his own acquiescence. There isn't much we can make him do. We're paper tigers. Behind all the bluster, we're shrimpy wizards, frantically pulling levers, bellowing into microphones, blowing smoke.

"Who made you the boss of me?" he asks.

The question almost makes me want to forgive him his trespasses. I like the rhythm of it. I like it as a refrain in a song or a poem. I like it as a book title. I like it as a question that the rest of the world could be asking Emperor Bush right now. I like it, above all, because it explains the trespasses themselves.

For the first few years of life, little ones accept the family setup just as they find it: the parents run things. Makes sense. We're big and threatening, but we also provide comfort and care. Toddlers only seem to act defiant. In fact, they can't control their impulses.

An eight-year-old, though, is capable of genuine defiance. He is choosing to disobey and argue and sass because he needs to know what will happen if he does. He needs to know his limits and ours.

Ultimately—this week would be good—we hope he will realize that relationships, at least healthy ones, aren't about power after all. They're about cooperation and respect. No, he doesn't really have to do what we say because there isn't much we will do to him if he disobeys. Our greatest power, he is learning, is the power to withhold affection. Once he decides that life is not all that pleasant with everyone angry at him all the time, he'll shape up.

Since he is our youngest, we are under no illusions that his passage out of this "phase" will mean smooth sailing from here on out. Adolescence looms. All is not love, peace, and harmony between us and his big sisters.

The difference between the two teenagers and their little brother is that they are learning to pick their battles. They have figured out that they're likelier to get their way on something that really matters to them if they remain in our good graces the rest of the time. They may even be ready to concede that we are not arbitrary and capricious tyrants, though I doubt they would go so far as to say we know what we're doing.

The goal, in other words, is not an argument-free household. We just don't want to have to argue about everything.

Zen and the Art of Driver Training

APRIL 27, 2003

I am sitting in the passenger seat of my car trying to stay calm, patient, and positive.

That is because my sixteen-year-old daughter is sitting in the driver's seat with her freshly minted learner's permit.

We drove straight from PennDOT's driver's license center in Pleasant Gap to the parking lot of the Bryce Jordan Center for Lesson 1.

PennDOT offers these guidelines for the driving "tutor":

- stay calm, patient, and positive;
- don't overreact, shout, or criticize.

Though my wife is otherwise a calm person, we all agreed that putting Mother in the passenger seat and Daughter in the driver's seat would be like pouring a bucket of bleach into a bucket of ammonia. That is why I am the designated driver trainer. The challenge, as I see it, is to stay calm, etc., and not overreact, etc., while also keeping my eyes open.

We were planning to take the "mini" van—to a new driver it's mini compared to an aircraft carrier—but my wife beat us to it, so we're taking the plunge in the little car with the standard tranny.

Learning to drive a stick is simple—as long as you're not trying to get anywhere. Daughter lets out the clutch, hits the accelerator—and stalls. Repeatedly.

"I hate this car," she says vehemently.

Inwardly I'm saying, don't worry, by the time you're through with the clutch and the starter, the car will be headed for the scrap heap. Outwardly, of course, I remain "calm, patient, and positive."

Needing a break from dead starts, we work on turns. New drivers don't slow down enough going into a turn and wind up too far to the left. Then they overcorrect to the right.

"Slow-slow-slow-slow-slow-slow-slow," I say at the beginning of every turn.

"You're too close to the curb," I say at the end of every turn.

I say these things as calmly, patiently, and positively as I can.

Getting a feel for when and how much to brake and accelerate is important, obviously, but the hardest part of learning to drive is developing judgment: Can I enter this intersection without giving the other drivers heart failure? Is there room for me and the car that's coming toward me, or do I have to tuck in behind this parked car?

To practice making these decisions, we hit the streets. The problem with hitting the streets in a college town is sharing the road with college students. The problem with college students is that they ask themselves, "Can I make it?" but do not ask themselves, "Will I give the other drivers heart failure?"

One car almost broadsides us at Park and University. Another cuts us off at Park and Bigler. Before I begin overreacting, shouting, and criticizing, I bring Lesson 1 to a close.

Lesson 2: We take the aircraft carrier. After orbiting Beaver Stadium, we aim the car toward the Penn Stater. I tell Daughter to bear right. She bears left.

"We're getting on the expressway," I point out, calmly, patiently, positively.

We drive one exit without incident. But when we get off, Daughter doesn't slow down enough for the turn into Toftrees. Another aircraft carrier is occupying the side of the road we appear headed for.

"Slow-slow-slow-slow-slow," I say in my calmest possible voice.

The collision fails to happen. By the time we get to our street, my heart rate has returned to normal.

Then we go up on the curb.

Note for next time: continue working on shifting and turning—and on staying calm, patient, and positive.

Keeping the Streak Alive

MAY 18, 2003

Let us pause amid the pomp and circumstance of commencement weekend to praise those who run naked through the streets.

That is, as long as they don't harass anybody.

When I read that four Penn State students had been cited for participating in the annual Mifflin Streak, I wanted to assail the prudery of a society that believes it is "indecent" for humans to expose their flesh.

I wanted to remind everyone that all God's creatures come in two basic models, male and female. Each bag of bones includes the same standard equipment, and we all know what that standard equipment looks like.

I wanted to ask, what's the big deal?

Where's the harm?

First, though, I did my homework. I learned there is more to the Mifflin Streak than streaking.

The tradition, such as it is, dates to the mid-1970s, according to old newspaper stories. The idea then, as now, was to let off steam at the start of finals week. The male residents of Mifflin Hall would strip, run to the women's dorms, and exhort those within to show themselves naked at the windows.

Good, clean fun, defenders said. A ritual casting off of burdens. One of the fifty things you have to do before you graduate from Penn State.

Not everyone agreed. In letters to the editor and guest columns in the *Daily Collegian*, women in the dorms wrote that they felt threatened or intimidated by the chanting horde. Victims of sexual assault said it brought back horrific memories.

Then there were the crowds.

The number of streakers ranged from fewer than ten to more than fifty.

But there were always a lot more gawkers than streakers. Many of them were drunk. Some, said Penn State Police Supervisor Clifford Lutz, were community members who heard the streak was happening and came on campus to ogle naked women. Inevitably, there were fights and gropes and property damage.

All in all, Lutz said, "this was a tradition that needed to die."

Instead, it went dormant for a couple of years. This year, student organizers drummed up interest in reviving the streak via the Internet and word of mouth. A crowd showed up. So did the police.

Their concern wasn't public nudity per se. "If you want to streak across the IM fields in the middle of the night, scream at the moon and run back in your dorm," Lutz told me, "nobody knows and nobody cares."

What the police care about is controlling an unruly crowd. So why go after the streakers? Why not wait until somebody commits a more serious crime than "open lewdness" or "indecent exposure?"

By then, answered Lutz, the situation may already be out of control. Arresting the streakers was aimed at nipping riotous behavior in the bud.

In other words, the police would rather react too quickly than wait too long. Maybe I'm getting old, but I appreciated the logic of Lutz's argument. Crowd management is a tricky business.

At the same time, I always want the police to exercise maximum restraint. Whether they did so in this case, I can't say: I wasn't there.

But Lutz and I agreed on one thing: It's too bad there didn't seem to be a way for the streak to remain an innocent act. It had to be sexualized and vulgarized and publicized and scrutinized.

And so, death to the Mifflin Streak. Long live running naked in the middle of the night and screaming at the moon.

But it should not be a spectator sport.

Movie Dog's Last Reel

OCTOBER 5, 2003

Bop the Movie Dog is falling apart. At fifteen, his hearing is shot, his eyes are clouding over, and his back legs don't always hold up their end.

He is the only creature I have ever seen fall up the stairs.

When he tries to turn around in a tight space, he cracks his head into a wall or a chair. This is painful to see.

The worst was when I called him in from the back yard. Instead of running around to the porch steps as he had done every other day for the previous eight years, he tried the shortest distance between two points. One problem: the shortest distance between two points is through a wrought-iron railing. Prang!

These frequent conks on the head may explain why Bop stares into odd corners as if he has forgotten where he was going or what he was supposed to be doing. At such times, he has the perplexed look of a Thurber dog made flesh.

Back when he was in his prime, Bop had that uncanny canine ability to sense in his sleep that I was putting on my shoes—an operation that, as far as I could tell, made no sound whatsoever. Now, I practically have to send him an engraved invitation requesting the honor of his presence at a tree-and-shrub sniffing tour of the neighborhood.

Sometimes, when he gets up, he can't uncurl himself, with the peculiar result that his head and tail face the same direction.

Scofflaw that I am, I used to walk him without a leash, confident that he would come when called and only cross the street with permission. Now, though, if he isn't tethered to me, he loses track of where I am. He hears me only if I clap my hands really loud. He responds by going the wrong way. So, now we walk half a block on the leash.

Cleaning up after him used to be a simple matter. Now, I feel like the guy with the broom at the end of the parade on "Rocky and Bullwinkle."

With all these warning signs we are, of course, bracing ourselves for our dog's demise. Part of me says it's time: he's not enjoying life much these days, and, frankly, with his various ailments, we aren't enjoying him much, either.

But he's been with us longer than two of our three kids. When we got him, he was a ball of black-and-white fuzz (and a zealous chewer of toys and bedding). As he got older, he looked less and less like his Border Collie mum and more and more like the terrier that came in the night. Everyone said he looked like a movie dog.

When we moved to State College in 1995, the movie dog was so discombobulated that he began terrorizing our houseguests. That was when my daughter put a sign on the door warning visitors that "he has biten pepil but not very many pepil."

Finally, he settled down to a life of following us from room to room, getting in the way, praying for scraps, and dreaming vividly about herding sheep.

Now, he spends so much time in dreamland that we check to see if he's breathing. Meanwhile, two new puppies have landed in the neighborhood. I'm afraid they'll be contagious, like babies.

The rest of my family thinks 'tis common enough to get a new dog when the old dog dies.

Aye, says I, the gloomy Hamlet of the house. 'Tis common.

The Brats in the Frats

FEBRUARY 22, 2004

This was no time for sleep.
This was no time for beer.
This was no time for sloth.
There was sidewalk to clear.

All that deep,
Deep, deep snow,
All that snow had to go.

When a storm dumped
A foot on our town the other day,
We said, "Somebody has to
Clean all this away.
Somebody, SOMEBODY
Has to, you see."
Who were those somebodies?
My neighbors and me.

Well...
There we were
We were working like that
And then who should be no-shows
But the Brats in the Frats!
"Oh-oh!" we said.
"Don't you walk down the street,
You'll get snow in your shoes,
You'll get frostbitten feet."

And then we got ice.
This was no time to shirk.
We said, "Frats! You come out!"
But the frats wouldn't work . . .

The frats are all young.
The frats are quite strong.
The frats are quite numerous.
This was all very wrong.

So we asked Borough Council.
It has something called FINES.
Fines are so hard to get
You rarely see anyone get one, I bet.

"Fine Little Frat Alpha.
Fine Beta. Fine Gamma.
Fine Little Frats Delta, Episilon,
Zeta and Eta..."

But the frat boys just waited
For warm sun and rain
While the ice thawed by day
And at night froze again.

"We need Voom," we concluded.
"Let's give eBay a shot."
Now don't ask me what Voom is.
I just couldn't say.
But, without it, let me tell you,
We'll be slipping till May.

RIP, Bop the Movie Dog

JUNE 13, 2004

It had been a tough spring. Bop's back legs had quit. His eyesight was bad and his hearing was worse. To walk him, I had to lift or tug him to his feet, slide him across the floor, nudge or carry him down the porch steps, and drag him half a block. And then, of course, I had to get him back in the house. It wasn't fun for either of us.

Once the warm weather arrived, I thought it might be easier for all concerned to let him laze like a farm dog on the back porch or in the backyard most of the day, but you know how dogs are. He had his spot in the corner of the dining room and he couldn't settle down anyplace else. He was messing the house, messing the porch, and messing himself.

On the other hand, he was still eating well and still walking a little, once he got going. Maybe he'd hang on for another year. But should he?

When the vet told us it was time for his annual shots, we said it was time to talk about the shot to end all shots. The night before our appointment, we gathered the children to make sure everyone knew what might happen.

The vet made it easy for us. He asked if we thought Bop was getting any enjoyment out of his life. If Bop were an old man we could have asked him how he was feeling and what, if anything, he wanted us to do about it. Our best guess was that he wasn't happy. A year ago we were still playing that game where he'd freeze, then I'd freeze, then he'd tear around the yard like a dog possessed. Now he never even wagged his tail.

The vet told us that more people regret waiting too long than feel guilty about putting their pet down too soon.

It's scary how easy it is to kill a living creature. One minute Bop's toenails were clicking loudly on the examining room floor. Then came the injection, and he was gone, this muttly Border Collie cross that had been in our family longer than two of our three children.

For the next couple of weeks, morning and evening and every time we came home, I thought, now I have to haul this poor beast out the door, and then realized, no I don't. Condolence cards came from neighbors—I'd never seen a pet condolence card before—but really, I felt more relief than grief.

On my son's tenth birthday, we told the story of the day he was born, how we went out to dinner, all nonchalant because this was child number three, how we walked the halls of the birth center, how he was the color of blueberry yogurt at birth. At 2:00 A.M., mother and baby were asleep, and I still had to walk the Bopster. It felt like my dog and I were the only wakeful beings in the world.

We plan to put a brass plaque low on the wall in Bop's corner of the dining room with an inscription cribbed from a warning sign my daughter tacked to the front door when she was learning to spell:

Here lay Bop the Movie Dog.
1988–2004
He bit pepil but not very many pepil.

Welcome to the Diploma Store

FEBRUARY 20, 2005

To our valued customers: Here at the Diploma Store, we care about what our customers think. That's why, every time you purchase credit hours from us, we ask that you take a moment to answer a few questions about our service providers.

Two years ago, we decided that our journalism customers would get better value for their diplomas if they knew how to spell, punctuate, and string together words in ways that conform to the grammatical definition of a sentence. And so, we added a one-credit, one-evening-per-week grammar class to our product line.

Last fall, our provider, whom we'll call Russell Frank, called his 180 customers to order by 6:30 P.M. by playing a few notes on the harmonica. Then, in a catastrophic burst of candor, he said he was proficient at grammar, spelling, and punctuation, but not an expert. Weeks later, he reminded them of this disclaimer when he struggled to differentiate between "because of" and "due to," or "compared to" and "compared with."

Here, unedited, is a selection of his customer evaluations:
What did you like best about the course?

- How it only met once a week.
- I hated it all.
- It taught me aspects of grammer I was unsure of.
- Snappy dressing teacher.
- Proffessor Frank explained everything well.

What did you like least about the course?

- The time, the memorization, the content. I'm not a big grammar fan.
- Dangling modifiers.
- Night class, profesor unsure of some answers.
- Nit picky stuff. Not fun.
- The book wans't worth $50.
- Slow-paced and dull.
- Too much stuff too fast.
- The exams were purposly tricky.

What suggestions do you have for improving this course?

- Get a teacher who knows the material and can find a better way to teach it.
- Instructor should play harmonica more.
- Have writing assinments.
- I think the tests had some rediculously hard questions.

Instructor's name:

- Russel Frank
- Frank Russell

To serve you better, we at the Diploma Store have extracted the following principles from these and similar evaluations of our other providers:

- There is no good time to purchase credit-hours. The sessions are always too early in the day or too late in the day.
- All credit-hour purchase sessions are too long.
- All instructional materials are boring and cost too much.
- All assignments are boring, take too long and are too hard.
- All presentations are boring.
- Any grade other than an A is unfair.

In light of the above, we proudly introduce the following changes in the way we do business: Starting in the fall, all of our courses will meet between 1:00 and 4:00 P.M. for fifteen minutes. In a typical class, customers will be asked to search the web for a good joke and then graded on their ability to forward that joke to a friend. Spelling will not count.

We understand that many of you will still find these classes inconvenient, long, difficult, boring, and unfair, but bear with us: our customer-service experts are studying the feasibility of converting from a credit-hours system to a credit-minutes system. Look for us to roll out a five-minute concept course next spring.

As for Provider Frank, he has been reassigned to train our other providers to develop snappier wardrobes and play the harmonica.

Thanks for shopping at the Diploma Store.

Things Fall Apart

APRIL 17, 2005

Then there are days that begin like this: Six o'clock. Time to wake up and smell the newsprint. I aim myself at the front door, turn, pull, and the doorknob comes off in my hand.

I am on one side of the door, the paper is on the other. To get it, I have to go out the back door, barefoot, bed-headed, and eccentrically attired and walk from back to front, in plain view of the neighborhood's early morning fitness fiends. Well, what's a little public humiliation to a newspaper columnist?

I wish I could tell you I then discovered that I had locked myself out and, like Fred Flintstone, bellowed my wife's name and rousted the rest of the neighbors from their beds. But life is rarely that cartoonish. What really happened didn't actually happen next, but three days before: the garbage disposal quit. The only reason I bring up its demise is that it only takes two or three little malfunctions to feel like your whole life is falling apart.

Somehow we made it to Saturday morning without barbarian hordes ransacking our unlocked house. (I would have pelted them with eggshells and grapefruit rinds.) Brimming with a weekend warrior's confidence, I stripped all the hardware off the door, which consisted of a half-dozen doorknob-and-dead bolt-related items, the lock mechanism itself, and about fifty thousand screws.

Have you ever exposed the inner workings of an old door lock? Don't. It's kind of like the moment when the Nazi raider lifts the lid of the lost ark. Your face doesn't melt, but you'll wish it did. For you will then spend the rest of your glorious Sabbath trying to put it back together, visiting locksmith shops that are inexplicably closed on the busiest home repair day of the week, reflecting on the utter uselessness of your doctorate when it comes to mechanical contrivances, resisting the urge to fling the whole works through the dining room window, and cursing your ill luck to live in a society whose members are so untrustworthy that we have to devote vast amounts of brain power to the design and manufacture of locks.

The real culprit was a tiny, wishbone-shaped spring. Each time my big, fat, stupid, clumsy fingers got the spring positioned correctly, the spring popped off and hid itself amid the complex patterns of the dining room rug. This happened approximately seventy thousand times. If my son didn't have a Little League game to get to, I'd probably still be at it.

Well, it turns out I was trying to play a concerto for four hands with two. That evening, my friend Tom came over, eager to be of use. With him holding everything in place while I bolted the two halves of the assembly back together, we got lock and knob and screws back in the door between dinner and dessert.

So now there's just the garbage disposal unit. And the three missing wheel covers from the minivan. And switches that don't switch and drains that don't drain. Chipped bricks on the front steps. Rust on the wrought-iron railing of the back porch. Cracks in the driveway. Bald spots on the lawn.

Junk in the garage. Junk in the basement. Junk in the attic.

And any day now, the carpenter ants will resume chomping and reduce the house to a pile of dust.

It's a bad sign when your 4:00 A.M. thoughts arrive in the middle of the day. Could be worse, though. The house and I are almost the same age. I could be obsessing about my own personal rust and bald spots.

Liberals on the Loose

MAY 2, 2005

A recent study reconfirms what everyone already knew: America's colleges and universities are hotbeds of liberalism.

The study, funded by the Randolph Foundation, described by the *Washington Post* as a "right-leaning group," found that 72 percent of us academics describe ourselves as liberals and 15 percent of us are conservatives.

Such numbers make it easy to leap to two conclusions, both of which, I believe, are unwarranted. The first is that politics plays a role in the hiring of faculty members. The second is that colleges and universities are liberal indoctrination centers.

During my seven years on the faculty of Penn State, my academic college has hired a dozen new people on the tenure track. As a member of the search committee and as an interested party, I have reviewed stacks of curriculum vitae and have attended hours of "job talks" by candidates for our positions.

I can't think of a single instance where it was obvious from the applicant's CV or presentation which party this person belonged to, or for whom he or she voted in the last election.

Of course, this evidence is anecdotal and limited to my own limited experience.

I have no idea what kinds of considerations come into play at other institutions, but my college offers courses on subjects such as the regulation of the airwaves, the content of prime-time TV shows and Hollywood movies, and press bias. Clearly, politics plays a role in discussions of these topics, and it would be hard for instructors to conceal their positions on these issues, assuming they even thought it was important to do so.

So if my college is not applying litmus tests to our job candidates, it's hard to imagine the math department doing so.

As for the indoctrination question, politics can pop up anywhere in the classroom. A meteorology class may take up global warming. An art history class may discuss the artifacts lost in the immediate aftermath of the American invasion of Iraq. A health and human development class on aging can scarcely avoid pondering proposed changes in Social Security or Medicare.

Still, politics narrowly defined as the positions one takes along the liberal-conservative continuum on state and national issues is going to be tangential at best to the subject matter of most college courses.

But even in classes like my journalism ethics class, where we talked a fair amount last fall about coverage of the presidential campaign, it is not a given that the instructor will try to impose his views on his students.

The belief has taken hold about college instructors and reporters alike that bias is an uncontrollable force: if you personally favor one side over the other on, say, the Terri Schiavo story, you simply cannot help slanting your coverage toward your own side.

This is nonsense.

Unless you're a total zealot—a description that fits few people—it's not that hard to set your beliefs aside, especially when it is considered unprofessional to do otherwise.

But let's say you do not feel obliged to set your beliefs aside in the classroom. I confess that my students had no doubts about how I was going to vote in the November election. That doesn't mean I bullied them.

Indeed, having tipped my hand, politically, I took pains to assure them that they could disagree with me and that I could not imagine any scenario where their political views would affect their grades in the course.

And even if I wanted to convert my students to my way of thinking, I doubt I would succeed.

The *Post*'s story notes that the academy has been shifting leftward for two decades—plenty of time for our ideas to have taken hold among vast numbers of college-educated citizens.

Yet the *Post* also reports that a recent Harris poll found that 18 percent of the general public describes themselves as liberal, compared with 33 percent who say they're conservative.

And as you may have noticed, the Republican incumbent, not the Democratic challenger, was re-elected last November.

At most, academic liberals are offering their students a critique of the dominant ethos before they go in search of jobs in corporate America. If even that amount of politicking worries conservatives, they should be aware of what anyone who makes a living in the classroom knows all too well: most of our students don't listen to a word we say.

The Invisible Poor

SEPTEMBER 11, 2005

It is the winter of 1938–39 and George Orwell is exploring the city of Marrakech in French Morocco.

In the public gardens, he feeds a bit of bread to a gazelle. A worker "looked from the gazelle to the bread and from the bread to the gazelle, with a sort of quiet amazement, as though he had never seen anything quite like this before. Finally he said shyly in French: 'I could eat some of that bread.'"

When Orwell passes a tiny old woman carrying an enormous load of firewood, he realizes he has crossed paths with such old women for weeks without noticing them.

"In a tropical landscape," he concludes, "one's eye takes in everything except the human beings . . . when the human beings have brown skins, their poverty is simply not noticed."

More than a half-century later, Hurricane Katrina revealed that the poor are still mostly invisible to us and that they still have brown skins. In a country where middle-class families own cars and take vacations and own houses and can buy whatever article of clothing or electronic device they simply must have, we find it hard to understand why some people in New Orleans didn't evacuate when they were told to do so. We have to be reminded that there are Americans who have no cars and no credit and no money in the bank.

Suddenly, we're appalled, just as we were back in 1998 when some white guys in Texas chained a black man to the back of their pickup and dragged him down a country road until parts of his body fell off. Racism and poverty in America? Still?

Middle-class prosperity shields us from hunger and thirst, from heat and filth, from danger and humiliation—all the discomforts and privations that afflicted the Superdome evacuees. We say we're starving when we haven't eaten since breakfast or that we're burning as we walk from the air-conditioned car to the air-conditioned building.

We know we're lucky. We know we should be thankful. Four years ago today, we got a searing reminder of the thinness of the membrane that protects us from harm. But apart from removing our shoes at the airport, how have our lives changed?

Over Labor Day weekend, back from our summer travels, we shook our heads at the human suffering and the official bungling and contemplated the great questions: Should we go to Ben & Jerry's or to the Creamery? Should we replace one of our ten-year-old cars, or sit tight a while longer? Should we be happy that Penn State won or worried that it didn't win more convincingly?

Such questions are both obscene and understandable. For even as catastrophes demonstrate the fragility of individual lives, they testify to the resilience of our way of life. Conflicts smolder and flare, the economy expands and contracts while I, a member of the great middle class from the day I was born, have slept all my nights in soft beds, except when I chose to "rough it" in the woods.

Sure, it can all come crashing down tomorrow. Mostly, though, it doesn't. And so we spend our days trying to be happy.

It is late in the summer of 2005 and I am moving my daughter into her dorm for the start of her freshman year in college. Hurricane Katrina makes landfall that same morning.

We are like Orwell's Europeans in the colonies, enacting the dramas of our privileged lives amid the cataclysms of the wider world.

Meet the Woo People

OCTOBER 9, 2005

Ten years ago this month, my family went to live among the Woo people of Central Pennsylvania. Here is what we have learned about their lifeways.

The Woo take their name from the exultant cries that pierce the Wooland night, which is when the Woo are most active. It is not entirely clear what these cries mean, but they have been variously translated as, "Behold, I have drunk many fermented beverages," and "Rejoice, for our champions have vanquished their opponents on the field of ritual combat."

Membership in Woo society appears to be of short duration, beginning only after they have left the homes of their parents and before they have sold their labor to the highest bidder. During this passage from childhood to adulthood, the Woo live in large groups segregated by sex, though it is not uncommon for an early morning walker to see a woman exiting one of the men's dwelling houses in clothing typically worn during nighttime festivities. The woman's journey back to the women's dwelling houses is known as the "Walk of Shame."

Curiously, whereas the men dress in clothing that is too large for them and conceals the contours of their bodies, the women wear garments that are too small for them and reveal the contours of their bodies.

In cool weather, Woo of both sexes wear hooded vestments that in some cultures signify membership in religious orders but among the Woo bespeak only their affiliation with either a diploma or a textile mill.

Both sexes also frequently wear caps equipped with visors designed to shield their eyes from the fierce Central Pennsylvania moonlight. The men, however, frequently wear their visors turned toward the back of their heads or off to the side, which according to some scholars, demonstrates the impact of excess consumption of fermented beverages on small motor skills. Others believe that the visors are vestigially functional, which is to say, merely ornamental.

Woo life is characterized by an abundance of festivity. During the daylight hours, the Woo play games that involve the tossing of the shoes of horses or the inflated skins of pigs. These games are made more challenging by the ritual consumption of fermented beverages.

At night, the Woo festivities begin in earnest. These revels sometimes generate friction between the Woo and the non-Woo residents of the Woolands, most of whom are diurnal. Generally, these tensions are managed through a tacit agreement that Woo festivities will be limited to the two nights of the week preceding their neighbors' days of rest. When festivities are held on other nights of the week, the neighbors call upon uniformed peacekeepers whose mere arrival in the Woolands causes the Woo to promptly lower the volume of their music.

(The Woo do most of their sleeping in the daytime under the tutelage of elders who have been trained to facilitate sleep by droning pleasantly for fifty to seventy-five minutes.)

Other contentious issues between the Woo people and their non-Woo neighbors center on the speed at which the Woo drive their chariots on Woolands byways, and their strong aversion to removing snow from the pathways in front of their houses. The Woo people, for their part, do not seem to be aware that their neighbors exist.

Outsiders believe the neighbors must be mad to dwell among such a boisterous people. The neighbors do not dispute this surmise. Occasionally, they will emit loud "woos" of their own, which are best translated as, "If you can't beat 'em, join 'em."

Leaf Ballet

The knock on Shingletown Gap is that it's too popular: it takes about fifteen minutes to pay your bill at the Corner Room and drive to the trailhead at the end of Mountain Road. But that's what I like about it.

On weekday mornings, my friend Dorn and I have been taking short walks through the woods between the Penn State campus and Toftrees, on the Orchard Park bike trail, through Millbrook Marsh, and through Walnut Springs Park. Each place has given us something lovely to look at: a city of mushrooms, like little tufa towers, in Walnut Springs, rippling water in Millbrook Marsh, and everywhere, the play of light and shadow, and the long ballet of leaf fall.

But these are tiny islands of green space. Every walk has brought us close to traffic or to heavy equipment. The Shingletown Trail took us away from traffic and into the silence of flowing water and another sound I had never heard before.

Our hike began in shade and in frost. Above us, the rocks glowed. Dorn, with his keen filmmaker's eye, kept wanting to stop. At first I was impatient. Let's walk a while, I thought, generate a little body heat. We'll gaze when we're warm. Soon, though, I stopped behaving as if I were driving through the landscape and started to look and listen.

So much to see, suddenly. At one bend in the creek there were ripples in the current as the water flowed around the rocks. The reflection of tree and sky on the surface. The creek bed below the surface. One brown trout.

Change focus the way you do to see the image within the image in a "Magic Eye" book and you see something else altogether. Change places, and the scene changes again. Stay put, and the light changes.

I felt like I could spend the day learning the discipline of seeing from this one spot. In fact, I felt like I should—not this spot, necessarily, and not this day, but any spot, once a month or once a season or once a year, like fasting on Yom Kippur: ritual attention-paying, to remind me that the world is saturated with beauty.

We moved on, of course. The sun blazed white-hot on the shiny surface of a rhododendron leaf. I held out my arms to the light like a child stepping out of the bath and into his mother's waiting towel.

Off the trail a little way we found iced-over puddles. I wanted to smash them because of how much I like that crunchy little sound, but Dorn talked me out of it by talking me into gazing at the texture and pattern of the ice.

I, in turn, talked Dorn out of his regret that he hadn't visited these woods two weeks ago when the colors were more vivid. It's like an oral history project, I told him. Whenever you show up, you're too late: the people who really knew the history are dead.

A puff of wind, and more leaves let go. Their flights remind me of ice-dancing routines. Some come down in tight spirals. Some swing through long, lazy arcs. Some seem to dance to music that no one else can hear.

I have always loved this spectacle. But in the quiet of Shingletown Gap, I heard for the first time the sound an oak leaf makes when it bumps twigs and trunks on its way to the ground—a sound like the tick of an old pocket watch.

All the Classroom's a Stage

JANUARY 13, 2008

Beginnings and endings. That's what I love about academic life. By the end of the fall semester, I was ready to wring necks. About half the students in my newswriting class misspelled Senator Clinton's first name in their last story. In journalism, this is not OK.

Now, though, everyone has a clean slate. And with hope springing eternal, I ask you students to bring a new mindset to the new semester.

Here's the idea: Most of you, I believe, come to class expecting to be spectators. The person standing at the front of the room is going to perform, and you are going to watch—or daydream or nap or discretely text message—just as spectators feel free to do at a concert or a play.

This model might make sense in the lecture hall. But it's all wrong for the classroom and the computer lab. In those smaller venues, you too are the performers. When you fail to show up, or show up but fail to contribute your energy, your interest, or your insight, you hurt the class as surely as an actor or a player who sits out or just goes through the motions hurts the rest of his cast or team.

You also forfeit your right to complain about being bored by a long-winded professor when you are making the prof do all the talking because you are not doing any of the talking. Perhaps most of you are just shy. Perhaps if I asked each of you instead of all of you if you got anything out of today's reading assignment, you'd have plenty to say; you just don't like to volunteer.

Fair enough. I'm reluctant to put people on the spot, but maybe I shouldn't be. Sometimes we need and even secretly want to be put on the spot. But how lovely it would be if some of you came to class bursting with questions or comments. How lovely it would be, in other words, if more of you walked in the room looking like you wanted to be there, or at least wanted to get something out of it, and therefore were prepared to put some effort into it.

Instead, as I circulate the room, I see your not-quite-suppressed smiles when you have just received an amusing text message on your cellphone. I hear keystrokes as you switch from Facebook or e-mail to the course website when I approach your aisle.

Here's what you don't get about such behavior:

First, we profs see you. You're not nearly as anonymous or invisible as you think you are.

Second, texting, messaging or web-surfing during class is rude, and it's the kind of rudeness that bespeaks immaturity. This is not how grown-ups behave.

Third, it distracts your instructor.

Fourth, it distracts you. You are supposed to be world-class multitaskers. I don't buy it. When you're reading or typing while I'm talking, you're not listening to what I'm saying. That's obvious when you turn in work and I see that you failed to do what I told you to do (or did exactly what I told you not to do).

I am sorely tempted to mark you absent when I catch you doing things unrelated to the work at hand because, in a very real sense, you are not present at such times.

None of this is to say that we profs couldn't do a better job of presenting our material and getting you involved. But the classroom isn't a theater or an arena or a ballpark. If you're expecting to watch a performance, better suit up.

Like all performers, we are only as good as our supporting cast.

The Flower Within the Flower

MAY 11, 2008

At a time of day when respectable people are gainfully employed, Dorn and I are walking around a quiet cul-de-sac. A red-haired woman in Nittany Lion navy emerges from one of the houses. We bid her good morrow. She returns the greeting.

"Are you inspectors?" she asks.

"Indeed, Madam," we sort of say, "we are inspecting the tulips." We are also assaying the ornamental fruit trees, registering the fragrance of the lilacs, and gauging the greenness of the grass.

'Twas my daughter, the aptly named Rosa, who got us into the flower-inspection business. She showed me how you cannot tell from the outside of the tulip what color you are going to find on the inside of the tulip: you have to peer in.

Poke your nose into a shocking pink one and you see a pale blue star at the bottom—the flower within the flower. Gaze into a yellow one and you glimpse the fire pit at the center of the world.

Seeking to learn more about tulip innards, I visited a web page supported by an ad that asks, "What does your soul look like?" I think I just found out. It looks like the inside of a tulip.

Normally, Dorn and I walk in the woods. But now, at the blink-and-you-miss-it peak of spring, we want to see the marriage of nature and art in our neighbors' yards. So we're doing town walks, which are more sociable than woods walks.

We've been invited to sit on Tom's porch and to heft the sword Ming bought in China. With Pam we mull the latest primary results. With strangers we agree that is it a beautiful day. And Dorn must greet all the giddy dogs and cautious cats.

Above all, there have been the lollipop farms of tulips, the blossom-blindness induced by pear and dogwood, the bleeding hearts that look more like Mexican folk art than like actual flowers, and lilac scent so powerful that you smell it before you see it.

At spring's peak, I think of William Steig, who in his *New Yorker* covers and children's book illustrations revealed himself to be a great lover of spring. In *The Singing Bone*, Pearl, a pig in a pink dress and bonnet, wends her ecstatic way home from school through a landscape in full bloom. "I love everything," she says.

The idyll doesn't last, of course. Pearl is waylaid by a dapper fox who plans to make her his main course at dinner. And back in the real-time world we must bear witness to spring's passage from the yellow phase of daffodil and forsythia to the pastel phase of the fruit trees and on to the deepening colors of the turn to summer.

Last weekend, the blooms withstood a downpour heavy enough to flood basements. The adhesives and juices that bind petal to stem and keep the whole works from toppling over were at full strength. The next day, the stems looked muscular, the petals tightly wrapped.

But by midweek, the petals look like old clothes, loose and frayed, no longer able to conceal the inner flower from view. In one College Heights yard, red petals lie on the ground, as lurid as battlefield carnage. In another, we see our first irises. And the pear blossoms are flurrying like warm snow.

When this mad carnival is over, Dorn and I will probably go back to the woods. But if you see a couple of shady-looking characters walking down your street in the next week or so, it's just us, the flower inspectors. This is our busy season.

In Defense of Those Pesky Gen Eds

OCTOBER 2, 2009

It's a simple transaction: if you, high school graduate, get passing grades in about forty classes*, we, the university, give you a fancy certificate attesting to that fact.

The certificate is valuable in two tangible ways: it can get you in the door at many workplaces, or, if you're a real glutton for punishment, it can boost you onto the next rung of the educational ladder.

On this we can all agree. But then there's that asterisk. It means that you can't just take whichever forty classes you like. We want you to take certain kinds of classes. Specifically, we want more than a third of your classes to reflect "Penn State's deep conviction that successful, satisfying lives require a wide range of skills and knowledge."

Implicit in this requirement is the belief that there is more to undergraduate education than job training. The General Education requirement—Gen Eds on the street—"augments and rounds out the specialized training students receive in their majors and aims to cultivate a knowledgeable, informed, literate human being."

So what do we mean by a knowledgeable, informed, literate human being?

When I was growing up, my big sisters used to talk about their Cit-Ed classes. I heard it as Sid-Ed. I had no idea what it was. Eventually I learned it was short for Citizenship Education, aka Civics. By the time I got to the grades where the curriculum went beyond the three R's, it was called social studies, which was mostly history.

Cit-Ed was where you were supposed to learn things like how a bill becomes a law, the differences between criminal and civil trials, the checks and balances among the three branches of government, and whether the Electoral College is a good party school.

Cit-Ed was also where you learned that in a democracy, public officials work for the people and not the other way around. This means that like any employer, we have a right—nay, a responsibility—to keep tabs on whether the folks whose salaries we're paying (through our taxes) are doing a good job. This is where journalism enters the picture.

If you don't know how government is supposed to work (via Cit-Ed), and you don't pay attention to how government is actually working (via the news media), you cannot be counted upon to vote intelligently or to separate lies and rumors (President Obama is a foreign-born Muslim-socialist-communist-fascist who wants to establish death panels that will decide whether Granny lives or dies) from fact. So the practical value of Cit-Ed makes it a no-brainer.

The humanities are a tougher sell. The university's explanation of the Gen Ed requirements touts the importance of "a familiarity with the cultural movements that have shaped societies and their values; an appreciation for the enduring arts that express, inspire, and continually change these values."

I completely agree, but then, I was an English major, which meant that I liked to read and write. Most students, in my experience, do not. So what do we do? Ram the humanities courses down their throats because like 'em or not, they're good for you, like cruciferous vegetables? Or figure ramming stuff down people's throats is no way for them to acquire a taste for it?

As an educator, I'm torn. On the one hand, I want to say, hey, if all you want is vocational training, you've come to the wrong place. Find yourself a vocational school and quit moping your way through our classes. On the other hand, the public university is a lovely idea. It's predicated on the belief that higher education is so valuable and important that everyone, not just rich kids, should get in on the action.

But students (and parents) need to take that asterisk more seriously. Here, we educators could use a little help from the pundits and politicians. A column in last Sunday's *New York Times Magazine*, for example, asks, "How much does higher education matter?"—and answers the question solely in terms of the degree holder's earning potential.

"Earnings," writer Dave Leonhardt concedes, "may be a flawed measure of an education's value, but they're about the only tangible measure we have."

Granted, Leonhardt is an economics columnist, but this is the quantitative fallacy par excellence—the idea that if you can't measure it, you probably can't even have an intelligent conversation about it.

As long as the dominant view of higher education defines its value solely in terms of the education-jobs link or in global terms, the education-competitiveness link, we will continue to see a mutually frustrating disconnect between what the students want to get out of college and what we, the faculty, are trying to give them.

Sure, we want them to get good jobs and make heaps of dough and contribute to American competitiveness in the global economy. Above all, though, we want them to begin to acquire wisdom. They need it, and the world needs it.

The Pursuit of Liveliness

JANUARY 8, 2010

What does it mean to have a happy new year?

Back when everything in my life seemed more or less fine, I assumed everything was more or less fine in the lives of the people around me. After all, in a society where most of us can get food when we're hungry and drink when we're dry, warmth when it's cold and coolness when it's hot, what is there to complain about?

Those who aren't happy, I decided, are insufficiently appreciative.

It was only when life started knocking me around a little that I became aware that just about everyone I knew was coping with something hard. Even when food, water, and shelter are givens, the sense of well-being that we derive from some combination of health, satisfying relationships, and satisfying activity, is not.

We who are middle-aged, for example, are simultaneously watching our children struggle with the transition from adolescence to adulthood and our parents age and die. Back trouble is rampant among us. Cancers and heart conditions are surfacing. Marriages are fraying. We fret that our skills will become obsolete before we're ready to retire and that we won't have enough money to live on when we do retire. We dread an old age reduced to endless rounds of medical appointments, nagging aches and pains, inactivity, loneliness, and boredom.

Needless to say, our children and our parents have troubles of their own. When I saw this headline in the *New York Times* the other day—"On Human Happiness, and Why It's So Hard to Find"—I thought, well duh! Life's tough. (The *Times* story was about a PBS series called "This Emotional Life" that aired this week.)

Much of what I know about the nature of happiness I have learned from my daughter Rosa. When she was in high school, the question, "How was school today?" had no meaning for her. Or rather, it had too much meaning. To answer it truthfully, she would have to say something like, it was good for the first seven minutes of French class, then the next twenty minutes were kind of boring, then I didn't feel that great the rest of the morning because I hadn't eaten breakfast, then eating lunch made me happy, but then I felt tired, then I really enjoyed part of my history class . . . and so on.

Happiness, in other words, comes and goes and often co-varies with one's physical state: an uncomfortable person is usually a grumpy person. When I think of being happy, I think of moments. Moments when the light is particularly beautiful, or the air is particularly delicious on my skin. Moments when I really hear and really see, when I really connect with the people I am with. The beauty of these moments is that you don't have to be on a white sand beach to have them. They can happen anywhere.

Or imagine this: It is morning. You and the person you love are lying side by side. The light is pearly. A breeze ruffles the curtains. There is no noise. You are comfortable and calm: You feel like you are floating. You do not want to move and you do not have to. You can make it last.

And then you can't. Everything changes: light, temperature, sound. The body wants something else—food, a different position, a bathroom. You feel you ought to do something, go somewhere. The spell breaks. Your floating body returns to earth. You get up.

Once we've figured out what brings us the possibility of momentary happiness (Did I put that modestly enough?)—afterglow mornings, lively evenings with friends, lovely walks in the woods, or whatever brings you bliss, joy, contentment—we owe it to ourselves to put ourselves in those situations as often as possible: there's a good new year's resolution for you.

But even in a good year, happy moments are going to be as sporadic as they were during a typical day in Rosa's life as a high school student. In that sense, the pursuit of happiness is bound to make us unhappy.

So maybe happiness isn't quite what we're after. We probably spend most of our time feeling neither happy nor sad, but just kind of OK. In the OK state (and I don't mean Oklahoma) nothing especially memorable or interesting is happening. Life feels like it's drifting by—which is kind of scary, given the brevity of our sojourn here on planet earth.

In contrast, there's how we feel when we or someone we care about is going through a crisis. We become hyper-aware, hyper-engaged. We become more attuned, not only to our own emotional states and those of the people around us, but to beauty in nature, in music, in movies, in books. For better or worse, we learn a lot at such times. It's all oddly exhilarating. As one of the experts interviewed on "This Emotional Life" puts it: "The opposite of depression isn't happiness; it's vitality."

Certainly, few of us want to suffer or see others suffer just so we can feel alive. But as the senses dull and the routines deaden, it's little wonder that we crave intensity. The challenge is to find a way to experience it without lurching from crisis to crisis.

Tow Story

The tribal elders of the Woo people were in town last weekend. This was good news for those of us who live among the Woo (named for the shrill cries they emit during their nocturnal revelries): The presence of Woo parental units meant that the nocturnal revelries would be relatively staid affairs. I looked forward to a peaceful night in the Woolands.

I went out for a while and when I came back, there was a line of cars on my street that approached football weekend density. So impressive was this line of cars, in fact, that not even my driveway interrupted it. Yes, blocking the entrance to the little strip of asphalt that I call my own, was a sporty little fire-engine red number.

So I turned onto the next street and, finding plenty of parking there, wondered why the guy who had blocked me out hadn't done the same.

There were a number of things I could have done in this situation:

(A) I could have composed a stern, but polite note, set it under the driveway blocker's windshield wipers, and given him a couple of hours to get the hell out of my way;
(B) I could have expressed my displeasure via some well-placed swings of a baseball bat;
(C) I could have asked the cops to please have the offending vehicle towed away.

I chose option C, for reasons I'll explain later.

The borough police, whom I have found to be supremely responsive over the years, arrived forthwith. So, too, did the tow truck. And just as the tow truck was maneuvering the offending car away from the curb and I was moving toward my car so I could restore it to its rightful place in my driveway, the car's owner, an obvious frat daddy, came lumbering down the street.

"Hey, that's my car!" he cried as he huffed and he puffed and he rapped on his own fender to get the tow truck driver's attention.

Here I must confess that I experienced that least noble of emotions, schadenfreude, or pleasure in the misfortunes of others. I must further confess, shamefacedly, that Frat Daddy's rotundity made the sight of him charging down the street all the more amusing. It was not my finest hour.

Soon enough, the tow truck driver braked and Frat Daddy demanded to know why his car was being towed. "Because you were parked illegally," replied the tow truck driver.

The cop quickly intervened. "If you've got anything to say," he informed Frat Daddy, "say it to me."

"I didn't see a sign," Frat Daddy said to the cop.

"You were parked in a driveway," the cop informed him.

"I wasn't aware," Frat Daddy said, lamely.

Even if he was blocking a driveway, Frat Daddy didn't see why he had to be towed away. "You could have just told me," he said. "Why didn't you come find me?"

To his credit, the cop did not laugh in his face. "How was I supposed to know where you were?" he asked.

Lucky for Frat Daddy, the tow truck driver didn't just drive off with his car as I've seen them do in crueler towns. He unhooked, demanded payment of sixty dollars for his time, and called it even.

Which suited me fine. I retained enough empathy to appreciate how maddening it would be to watch your car being towed away at the very moment you had arrived to rectify the situation. And I thought sixty dollars was a reasonable price for Frat Daddy to pay for being too snockered or lazy or oblivious to park on the next block.

But let us probe this matter more deeply.

The case against Frat Daddy looks like this: What if I had been blocked in rather than out and had to, say, catch a plane? What if someone in my car was disabled and we needed to get the car as close to the house as possible?

The case against me looks like this: neither of the above scenarios was the case. Assuming I could get into my driveway before I wanted to go to bed (the borough tickets cars for parking on the street overnight), the inconvenience to me—having to put my shoes back on, having to go back outside—was slight. Even though Frat Daddy was clearly in the wrong, I could have cut him a break.

So why didn't I? Well, there's a little history here. A continuing source of irritation in the Highlands is the sense that the Woo people are oblivious to our presence among them. They believe the neighborhood is theirs; if the rest of us are displeased or inconvenienced by their behavior, well, we can go live elsewhere.

The presence of the hot red car at the entrance to my driveway seemed to epitomize that attitude. Houses that aren't fraternity houses? What houses? Neighbors who might want to park their cars in their own driveways? What neighbors?

Forgive me, but I wanted that sucker towed. Woo!

Straight from the Lion's Mouth

MAY 7, 2010

Man, am I popular all of a sudden.

Girls I don't even know are coming up to me and kissing me on the cheek. Some are putting their arms around my shoulders in a very familiar way. Some are even mounting me, if you'll pardon the expression. That is, they are climbing on my back and either straddling, side-saddling, or lying on their tummies, knees bent, feet pointing skyward, and ankles crossed in what I can only describe as a bearskin rug position.

Guys are getting pretty chummy with me too, though they skip the bearskin rug pose.

Here is what it was like to be me on a recent brilliant and breezy afternoon, oak leaf shadows dappling my tawny limestone hide:

A girl in a blue gown and a blue cardboard hat nestles against my left flank and cups my left ear with her right hand. She smiles so hard it looks like her face hurts, while her mother frames and focuses. Click.

Then Mom hands the camera to the next person in line and joins her daughter. Click. Then Mom reclaims camera and Daughter straddles me.

"It's slippery," she says.

"That's cute," says Mom.

Click.

"Next," says Mom.

Next is a quintet of red-, blond-, black-, and two brown-haired girls, all wearing white sleeveless dresses. They line up along my starboard side. Then they stand behind my port side and lean their arms on my back, looking like a row of blooms on a dogwood branch.

Then there are the couples. She drapes her arms around his chest, like a sash. He rests his hand on her knee. He sits on my left shoulder, she on my right, like driver and passenger in a car. They dismount by sliding down my nose.

A girl with blue toenails has brought an extra mortarboard—for me! I feel positively professorial. She puts her arm around my left front leg. Then she puts her hand on my right front paw. Then she kisses me on my left jowl, her tassel billowing in the breeze.

Next comes a sextet of girls. After they all pose in their caps and gowns, three pose with caps, no gowns and three with gowns, no caps.

A guy, his parents, and his aunt take their turn. Dad takes the pictures while the two women stand behind him, beaming. Then Dad gets in front of the camera. Then Mom does. Then Mom, Dad, Auntie, and Senior cluster around my head for a final shot.

A radiant blond leans against my head, crosses her arms, crosses her ankles, and cocks her head winsomely.

"Ride the lion," urges her radiant blond mom.

"I don't know if I can do that," the daughter says. She can, and she does. "Does my bra show?" she asks. It doesn't.

Some of my "riders" look like they've been going for gallops on the backs of lions since they learned to stand. Others hang on for dear life, as if afraid I'll buck them off—which I would never do.

A guy with a passing resemblance to Ralph Fiennes strikes an insouciant pose—right elbow on my left shoulder, left hand on his hip. Then he straddles my neck, a hand on each ear as if they were handlebar grips. Then he poses on my back with one knee down and one knee up, as if he's shot me on safari.

A mixed-gender septet, all the guys in aviator shades, climbs aboard and arranges itself as the crew of a Viking longboat. The guy at my "bow" mimes horns with his fingers. Everyone else pretends they're rowing.

For his solo shot, the Viking slides between my front paws so that most of him is under me except for his head, which dangles off my pedestal. He explains that I am supposed to look like I am mauling him, which, of course, is another thing I would never do.

Then he strikes a solemn pose. "Get a Mom shot," he says to his crew.

Only one couple gives up. "Let's try the JoePa statue," the girl says.

Lest I feel slighted, two girls position themselves on each side of my head, pucker up, and kiss me on the jowls.

"Seniors!" someone shouts from a passing car in a falsetto voice.

Apart from the pair that forsakes me for JoePa, I'm impressed by how patient and polite everyone is. Even without velvet ropes or ushers, everyone stands in line. The picture takers apologize for taking too long. The people in the queue urge the picture takers to take their time.

"It's only gonna be a few hours," one joker says.

Everyone agrees to take photos for everyone else so everyone in every photo party can be in the picture.

"You've got to get a picture with the lion," a senior explains.

I've Sneezed and I Can't Get Up

JUNE 11, 2010

I made the mistake of sneezing the other day.

I had driven my son to the Babe Ruth fields for a game. While the kids warmed up, I settled in at a picnic table with a master's thesis I had to read (see, we profs do too work in the summer). Then came the tickle in my nasal passages.

What an odd coincidence to simultaneously sneeze and get shot in the back. At least it felt like I had been shot in the back. I tried to stand up. Couldn't. I rested and tried again. No go.

Ethan came over to hit me up for money for a sports drink. I told him what had befallen me, but not to worry: I'll relax, watch the ballgame, and after a while my pain-o-meter will dial down from agony to dull ache and I'll be able to get up. Ethan brought me a bag of ice from the snack shack, then returned to the dugout.

The ice helped—until I dropped it. I couldn't pick it up.

From time to time I tried, ever so gingerly, to lift myself up by pushing down on the bench or the table with my palms. Fuggedaboutit. I felt like a beetle struggling to right itself after being flipped over by a sadistic kid.

Was I going to have to call an ambulance? The alternative was to spend the rest of my life at the Babe Ruth complex. Could be worse:

First, there would be ballgames to watch, at least in summer.

Second, I had reading material (this was going to be the most carefully edited thesis in the history of graduate education).

Third, I was in a roofed picnic pavilion, which would afford some shelter from sun and rain.

Fourth, I could probably get someone to bring me an occasional burger or pretzel or soft drink from the concession stand—not the healthiest diet, but more palatable than the raw flying fish the Colombian seaman had to eat in Gabriel Garcia Marquez's *The Story of a Shipwrecked Sailor* (a book I recommend).

The thought of the other people at the ballpark brought me to my senses. I could do what all guys, in our dimwitted machismo, hate to do: ask for help.

Just then, I spied two friends and fellow Babe Ruth parents. I told them of my plight. Each offered an arm. I pulled myself up. Sean fetched ibuprofen from his car. Mike got me a new ice bag. They asked me if I could get home all right. I wasn't sure I could get into my car, or, once in it, if I could get out again. But I planned to try.

I got my butt into the driver's seat but couldn't figure out how to tuck my head under the doorframe. I got my head in but couldn't reach over to close the door.

Eventually, body in car and door closed, I was able to drive home. Disembarking, I unfolded myself as carefully as a person who opens a present and wants to reuse the wrapping paper.

Mercifully, I slept.

Next day, my doctor informed me that my sneeze had triggered a back spasm. Seems obvious now, but at the time I assumed I'd blown out a disk and would need to go under the knife. The doctor also set me up with a physical therapist. But that appointment was several days off. In the meantime, I went trawling for home back spasm treatments on the World Wide Web.

One site offered emergency back care. The video began with New Age-y music, which made me skeptical, but the exercises seemed worth a try: one simply relaxes the spastic muscle by lying on one's back, arching, and well, un-arching, repeatedly. To my amazement, I felt immediately better, though maybe that had more to do with the music ending than with the exercises.

Apart from frequent arching, the main order of business between the doctor's appointment and physical therapy appointment was stifling sneezes. Whenever I felt the telltale nose tickle, I grabbed the old schnozz and squeezed until the urge subsided or my head exploded, whichever came first. This was deeply unsatisfying, probably because a sneeze, at least according to folk belief, is like a mini-orgasm.

But the hardest thing about my delicate condition has been putting on my socks. Tying shoes is tough also. If I were smart I would go sockless and wear slip-ons, except that walking actually feels pretty good, and to walk I need more serious footwear.

Bike riding feels OK too, apart from getting on and off, which I have been doing by laying the bike flat on the ground.

Now that I've visited the physical therapist, though, cycling and running are out; press-ups and lumbar extensions and rolled-up towels between my back and my seat back are in.

On the bright side, I'm not living in the picnic pavilion at the Babe Ruth fields.

Stand-Up Guy Seeks Position

JUNE 25, 2010

I am writing this column standing up for the same reason I am doing everything standing up this week: I can't sit down.

No, I didn't get quilled in the backside by an angry porcupine. Nor did I fall asleep on a nude beach while lying on my stomach or squat on a red ant's nest. In fact my butt isn't bothering me at all. It's my left leg.

The trouble began three weeks ago with a sneeze that sent my lower back into a spasm. For the next week I watched pro basketball players, World Cup soccer players, and Broadway hoofers at the Tony Awards contort their bodies into preposterous positions while I could barely pull on my socks.

The week after that, I spent roughly half of a five-hour flight to California standing by a bulkhead reading a magazine like a rush-hour subway rider because it felt better to stand than to sit.

This week, the pain migrated from my back to my leg. You would think if your leg was bothering you that the obvious solution would be to take a load off. But for reasons a doctor might be able to explain if I could bear to sit in a car long enough to get to a doctor's office, the leg hurts worse when I sit.

Or lie down. As you might imagine, the inability to lie down has made sleeping rather problematic. The first night I may actually have dozed off horsey-style, while standing in the middle of the room. And I'm pretty sure I slept for twenty minutes or so while kneeling on the floor with my head on the bed, like a child who nods off during his nightly prayers.

Last night, after taking the PM version of an over-the-counter painkiller, I was able to sleep on my stomach for an hour or two.

But now it's daytime, and my mother raised me to believe that it is important to do something productive every day, so I'm trying to think of useful things I can do while standing around, apart from writing this column, that is. Some possibilities:

In the garden: Stand me up in the vegetable patch and you wouldn't see crows brazenly sitting on my shoulders and feigning fear of an obviously faux foe. Unlike the traditional straw-filled scarecrow, I could wave my arms and raise a ruckus. You could even have me double as a tomato stake or beanpole, though I don't exactly have a beanpole body (which is why I'm not proposing to rent myself out as an artist's model).

In the front yard: Dress me in silks and put a lantern in my hand, and I could be your lawn jockey. Stick me in a sunny corner, and I could serve as a sundial.

At a checkpoint: Looking to fill a sentry-level position at a border crossing or the entrance to a secure installation like a government building, gated community, bridge, or tunnel? I could be your Beefeater, credential checker, or toll taker.

In a museum: As a guard I wouldn't even need to take a break because I wouldn't sit down anyway.

On the highway: If your tax dollars are going to be used to pay road construction crews to stand around, you may as well hire a guy who isn't good for anything else.

On the street: I could perform a number of marketing tasks, including handing out flyers, hawking papers, and wearing a sandwich board.

On the movie set: Need extras to mill around in the background? I'd need very little rehearsing. These days, all I do is mill around.

In the home: Too tired to hang up your sport coat but afraid it'll get wrinkled if you toss it onto a chair? Just toss it to me and I'll put it on and wear it until the next time you want to wear it. I could also serve as a tie rack, towel rack, or laundry-drying rack. Not sure whether to hang the masterpiece over the sofa or the fireplace? I can spend half the day holding the painting in one location and the other half holding it in the other while you make up your mind. Just don't ask me to house-sit.

At the ballpark: During football games, I can be the guy who holds the sticks that tell what down it is. In baseball, I can be a first base coach (my injury does not prevent me from patting rumps).

In the classroom: Need a sub to stand in front of the room and babble at students who are not paying the slightest attention? Believe me, I have tons of experience.

Hire me and I promise you this: you'll never catch me lying down on the job or participating in any sit-down strikes.

Return of the Woo People

AUGUST 20, 2010

I was sitting on my back porch the other night when I heard two sounds that told me summer was over. One was the rumble of a rented truck. The other was the whooping of the occupants of the rented truck.

The Woo people were back in town.

If you're new to these parts, let me enlighten you. The Woo are a seminomadic people. From late August until early May, they take up residence here at the foot of Mount Nittany to receive instruction from elders like myself. From May to August, they return to the homes of their families to earn money to buy the fermented beverages they will need to dull the pain of receiving instruction from elders like myself.

The return of the Woo people was heralded by the stained and rancid sofas that sprouted curbside when their August 1 leases took effect, much as the sprouting of snowdrops and crocuses more prettily heralds the arrival of spring.

If you live near the lodging houses of the Woo people, you will surely hear them this weekend, for this interval before the onset of instruction is a time of reunion and rejoicing. Next weekend they will celebrate the end of the first week of instruction. The weekend after, they will celebrate the first ritual combat of the 2010 season.

The Woo people are great believers in celebration. In fact, so prodigious have their celebrations become that last year they gained national recognition as the greatest revelers in the land.

Now, though, the Woo people appear to have been one-year wonders. When Princeton Review announced its new top party schools rankings earlier this month, our Nittany Lion clan of Woo people had been surpassed by the Bulldog clan at the University of Georgia and the Bobcat clan at Ohio University.

Will the Woo people redouble their efforts to reclaim the top spot this year?

Last spring, their defiant observance of a second green beer festival (State Patty's Day) and an early Cinco de Mayo fiesta (Cinco de State) in the face of intense pressure not to add additional drinking-centered holidays to an already besotted calendar seemed to signal their determination to live up to their national reputation.

On the other hand, this year's lower ranking could mark the beginning of a more temperate era at the foot of the sacred mountain. After all, the rankings are not some kind of independent assessment by a panel of professional party-school evaluators, but a count of the number of students who voted for their own school. A smaller turnout among Penn State students is likelier to reflect some disenchantment with the party school reputation than with the party scene itself.

We will know more after this weekend. Listen for the howls—the "wooing" of the Woo people—in the wee hours of the morning. Check your lawn and shrubbery for Natty Lite cans. Scan the police blotter on Monday.

If it was loud, if there was a lot of beer trash, if there were a lot of public drunkenness/public urination/underage drinking violations, we may be in for another year of raucous partying.

If it was calm, perhaps all the scolding, all the ugly statistics and incidents associated with binge drinking have had a sobering effect. Let us hope so.

Last spring, I drew encouragement from the looks on the faces of the women in my class as they listened to the *This American Life* program devoted to the drinking culture at Penn State. When host Ira Glass noted that female fraternity party attendees were dressed like cocktail waitresses at a strip club, the thought balloons above their heads said, "Wow, is that what we look like?" I don't think they had ever thought about how they were perceived by others. They seemed embarrassed.

The other question before us is whether, absent an early tragedy like the drinking-related death of freshman Joey Dado last September, the university and the community will be reactive or proactive in regard to the culture of drinking unto sickness.

I vote proactive. Some months back I suggested that a delegation of neighbors pay a friendly visit to each of the fraternity houses at the start of the academic year to make the following simple point: this is a neighborhood and not some sort of free zone where one can make as much noise as one likes and use the adjacent yards and streets and alleyways as latrines.

I still think such visits are a good idea because trust me, it doesn't occur to the Woo people that they live in a neighborhood and are therefore expected to be neighborly, just as it doesn't occur to the women who attend their parties that they look like cocktail waitresses at a strip club.

Must You Go?

NOVEMBER 5, 2010

Let us now say a proper farewell to exquisite October. Last week I went with Dorn, my partner in flower and leaf inspection, on a last-chance foliage tour of College Heights.

We began in Sunset Park, where mothers pulling children in wagons glowed in the amber radiance of a sinking sun. I was sorry I no longer had little ones to take to the park until we got close enough to hear that the kiddies were fussing: this is the time of day when they get tired and hungry.

If only they could know that it was the most beautiful day in the history in the world! Wind and rain the night before had so thoroughly scrubbed and dried the air that every detail of every solid object seemed emblazoned against the sky. All this time we were unaware that we had been looking at the world through gauze.

Oak leaves, which had been merely brown the day before, caught fire in the afternoon light, leaping with deep yellows and oranges and surprising flashes of green. But the award for the most beautiful tree in College Heights went to a maple. If I had taken a photo, I could tell you what kind of maple; what I remember are leaves that were mostly red with orange veins. Or maybe mostly orange with red veins. In bestowing our award we weren't telling the householder anything he didn't already know. "It makes me happy every day," he said.

From College Heights we crossed the blacktop lane to the Penn State president's house for a tour of the H.O. Smith Botanic Gardens, which I hereby nickname the Hosbog. We stopped first at the Hosbog fountain, where I became as transfixed as Madison

Bumgarner in his dugout pitching trance in Game 4 of the World Series. I gazed until I could see the jets of water shatter into silver marbles before they fell. And as I walked away, it struck me that I like the fade-out sound of rushing water as I withdraw just as much as I like the fade-in sound of rushing water as I approach.

Day was fading to night now, just as brilliant October was fading to dusky November. It was like watching your lover leave the room. "Must you go?" playwright Harold Pinter asks historian Antonia Fraser when the two of them meet. Lady Antonia stays, and the two writers spend the next thirty years together. (*Must You Go?* is the title of her just-published memoir of those years.) October really must go, but before I went all melancholy about it, I thought of the drill-sergeant therapist in the TV commercial who proposes that he and his crybaby client "chug on over to namby-pambyland," and I bucked up.

After all, mushy as I'm sounding here, my mind, too, felt scrubbed and clear. And it wasn't just the weather that did it; it was walking with my fellow leaf inspector. Alone, I would turn inward and not notice. Dorn and I go on these walks with the express purpose of noticing. Indeed, sometimes our interaction consists of little more than pointing or saying, "Wow, look at that one." And after all that looking, I feel like I've plugged into a power source that keeps me energized for days.

Even when the calendar flipped to November and the cold wind blew and the baseball season ended and the last of the Reese's and KitKat bars disappeared from the trick-or-treat bowl, I found the confluence of cosmic and cultural order oddly satisfying. Next morning there was white rime on my neighbor's roof, and the cold must have fatally compromised the adhesive that binds leaf to twig, for all the remaining leaves were sashaying and spiraling ground-ward, especially the gingko leaves, which had waited and were now showering down one after another and forming a gold pool at the base of the tree.

The flight of some of the maple leaves traced the outline of a Christmas tree in the air, or if you can't see that, just swing your index finger in an arc while dropping your hand as if you were conducting an orchestra with that one finger. The golden shower of gingko leaves was Zeus coming down from Olympus to impregnate "rich-haired Danae," who bears Perseus, slayer of Medusa, as I was off to the polling place in the vain hope that I could vanquish President Obama's political adversaries with my one small vote.

Ah well. The political pendulum swings left and swings right, like the maple leaves. But color, light, and air are a steadier source of joy and strength.

Football's Terrible Beauty

Why do we love football?

According to some of the writers who have been covering the NFL's crackdown on head-cracking tackles, we love it because we are bloodthirsty savages who are thrilled by violence. Lose the violence, these commentators say, and you lose the audience.

I don't think this is true. I think we love football for the same reason we love art or ballet or the way an oak tree looks on a sunny afternoon in autumn: because it is beautiful.

Admitting that we respond to the beauty of football might be more embarrassing than admitting that we respond to the violence of football. Consider the hyper-masculine opening of every NFL telecast—the martial music, the basso profundo voice-over (the same voice that's used to sell rugged trucks and chuggable beers), the crashing and shattering helmets. It says: Never mind that you're all reclining in your La-Z-Boys and your Barcaloungers. You appreciate these tough guys because you're a bunch of tough guys yourselves. It doesn't say: you appreciate the balletic grace of these athletes because you are connoisseurs of beauty.

In fact, though, a football game, indeed, every sports event, is an aesthetic extravaganza, beginning with the field of play itself. A thousand baseball writers have rhapsodized on the symmetry of the diamond and the lush green color of the turf. The gridiron has a similar appeal.

I suppose an evolutionary biologist would tell us that suburbanites spend bazillions on lawn care and urbanites seek respite from the concrete canyons in city parks because green grass signaled abundant food and water to our food-questing ancestors. I suppose they'd say we respond to symmetry from the moment we set eyes on the symmetrical faces of our mothers as infants. In any case, we love the beauty of the field of play.

Then there is the beauty of uniforms: the brilliant colors and dazzling whiteness of jerseys, the shininess of helmets, the meaning-saturated letters and numbers and logos on jersey, helmet, and field. We're all typophiles—lovers of the symbol systems we use to order a wild world. Even Yankee haters concede that there are few things spiffier than those Yankee pinstripes and that interlocking NY logo. For proof that the sartorial is an important component of the sports experience, consider the howls of protest that greet attempts to add flair to the Nittany Lions' vanilla uniforms. Or go to Uni Watch on the ESPN website.

Above all, the pleasure of sport is the pleasure of seeing what trained and gifted athletes can do with the sack of muscle and bone that is the human body. The most thrilling plays in football aren't the bone-crushing tackles, but the sideline or back-of-the-end-zone catches. These are the plays where a receiver leaps, snatches the spiraling ball out of the air, and somehow manages to touch both toes in bounds before his momentum carries him out of bounds. It is a thing of beauty, as graceful as any choreographed move in the world of dance.

Also lovely:

- when a quarterback "threads the needle," throwing a pass to the exact and only spot he could have thrown it where it could be caught by his own guy and not by a defender;
- when a runner spins or fakes or accelerates in a way that leaves his pursuers grasping at air rather than at him;
- when a guy like Ben Roethlisberger completes a pass with pass rushers draped over him like wet laundry on a drying rack;
- when a guy like Adrian Peterson appears to be bottled up and then drags about a half-ton of human flesh another ten yards down the field, or breaks away from the pile altogether;
- when a guy like Troy Polamalu gets to the ball carrier not by going around people but by springing into the air and flying over them.

I suppose you could still have leaping catches and precision passes if pro football suddenly went from tackle to two-hand touch. Forget all these other moments, though: they're predicated on the need to tackle, or to break tackles. And when very large men "gallop terribly against each other's bodies," as the poet James Wright put it, terrible injuries are bound to occur.

But acknowledging our complicity in these injuries is not the same as rooting for them to happen. Which is why, when I read in the *New York Times* that violence "is the essential ingredient that attracts fans to football," or that it is "the NFL's primary product," I have to disagree.

When, on that beautiful expanse of green grass, an irresistible force in a shiny helmet meets an immovable object in another shiny helmet, I don't exult. I cringe.

How to Rein in the Woo People, Part 1

NOVEMBER 19, 2010

Glug, glug, glug. Yak, yak, yak.

They drink. We talk. And the quandary remains: how to address Penn State's drinking problem.

We, their neighbors, would like the Woo people to see the error of their ways. We want them to recognize that they share a neighborhood with us and to accept our desire, nay, our right, not to be disturbed by late-night ruckuses or dismayed by property damage when we greet the world in the morning.

Ain't gonna happen.

Knowing it ain't gonna happen, the hard-headed realists among us are calling for legal and extra-legal remedies: steeper fines from the state and steeper academic penalties from the university.

Sure. The problem with enforcement-centered approaches, though, is that they're predicated on arrests, and the chances of the police catching most late-night revelers in the act of snapping a fence post or howling at the moon are not good.

Of course, penalties are mostly supposed to serve as deterrents: if the Woo people know that running wild through the streets may lead to getting booted out of school or incurring the wrath of their fine-paying parents, they may become more temperate in their habits.

Ah, but as the hard-headed realists have pointed out at the many meetings I have attended, deterrence presupposes an ability to consider the consequences of one's actions. A person who is on his second or third can of Four Loko does not possess this ability.

So if appeals to their better natures aren't going to work, and threats of punishment aren't going to work, what's left? My answer: make school harder.

College students party with such gusto in part because they view their undergraduate years as a last hurrah. Party now because once you have to be at your post at 9:00 A.M. ready to make, market, or trade those widgets for the next eight hours, you flat-out will not be able to drink late into the night.

Implicit in this line of thinking is that as a student you don't have to be anywhere early most days, if ever, and you're not going to have to work all that hard for all that long throughout the rest of the day. One of the dumbest moves Penn State has made in the years I've been around here has been the "student-centered" shift away from morning classes.

The argument that early classes conflict with late-adolescent bio-rhythms is a bizarre one if only because most kids have been getting up for school somewhere between 7:00 and 8:00 A.M. their entire lives.

And if the argument is that students won't come to 8:00 and 9:00 A.M. classes, the rebuttal is the same: they showed up when they were in high school, didn't they?

And why? Because attendance was compulsory.

I didn't take attendance when I started teaching. That's baby stuff, I thought. These kids—OK, their parents—are forking over all this dough to come here. If they want to waste the money and forego exposure to my modest expertise, it's their choice and their loss.

Besides, who wants to look out at a sea of surly sleepyheads who are present only under duress? I've even heard colleagues cast voluntary attendance in terms of pedagogical challenge: their job is to make their classes so entertaining that students want to be there.

I see things differently now. First of all, not taking attendance sends the unmistakable message to students that what goes on in the classroom isn't terribly important. It's what enables them to ask that most maddening of questions when they're absent: "Did we do anything in class yesterday?"

Incidentally, allowing students to add classes two weeks into the semester sends the same message. Oh, they can catch up on the readings and whatever assignments they missed, but those first couple-three introductory lectures? Gone, but no biggie.

The second reason for an attendance policy is that it's inherent in the idea of credit hours. When you register for a three-credit course, you are registering for three hours of instruction per week. Getting credit for those three hours begins with actually being there in the classroom.

Fine, the attendance-optional instructors may say. You want to take attendance in your own classes, go right ahead. But I contend that students construe the existence of any attendance-optional classes as proof that attendance doesn't really matter (if it did, everybody would require it) and therefore, instructors who take attendance are petty tyrants.

Make 'em all come to class, I say.

Next week I'll talk about the need to make school harder by giving students more work. The argument so far: more morning classes and compulsory attendance will do more to discourage binge drinking than zealous law enforcement on the street and stiffer penalties imposed by the courts, the legislature, or the Office of Student Affairs.

How to Rein in the Woo People, Part 2

NOVEMBER 26, 2010

Penn State students binge-drink for the same reason dogs lick their private parts: because they can.

That is, they can drink late into the night because they don't have to get up early for class and because their classes aren't all that demanding.

Therefore, one way to curtail the drunkenness that disturbs the peace, stresses law enforcement and emergency medical personnel, and busts the borough's budget is for the university to demand as much dedication from full-time students as employers demand from full-time employees.

Last week I wrote in favor of early classes and a university-wide compulsory attendance policy. This week I'll address grading and workload.

Let me concede right off that I do not know whether courses across the university have gotten easier over time—whether students are doing less work for higher grades. But judging from all the "playing" I see in my neighborhood at all hours of the day and night, and from the quality of the work I get from my students, my sense is that Penn State students do not spend a lot of time on schoolwork.

They'll dispute this, of course. When my own students complain about a grade that should have been much lower, they sometimes voice their dismay by telling me how hard they worked on the travesty in question. I want to ask, "What does working hard even mean to you?" because I suspect the honest answer is something like "Twenty minutes of sustained effort" (while texting and iPodding, of course). They're automatic writers most of them. First thought, best thought, as Allen Ginsberg said. Revise? Proofread? Nah, good enough. If only their first thoughts were as good as Ginsberg's.

Perhaps you're thinking, well, if the work's that bad, flunk 'em. Ah, but if we gave Fs to every assignment we thought deserved an F, I'm telling you, we'd be flunking students left and right. It would be interesting to see what would happen if we started giving students the grades we thought they deserved, but frankly I don't think most of us have the guts.

Two things discourage university instructors from being as rigorous as we should be. One is that the more work we give our students, the more work we make for ourselves. Ask anyone on the faculty and he or she will tell you: the worst part of the job by far is grading papers. Ask them if they would rather spend ten hours grading essay questions or ten minutes grading multiple-choice questions and the other nine hours and fifty minutes on their own research, and it's a no-brainer.

Then there are the dreaded SRTEs—the student evaluations. Though students are asked to judge the quality of a course, it stands to reason that many will feel more kindly disposed toward an instructor who didn't make them work too hard. In my own case, I've always been amused by complaints that a class was too long or that there was too much reading. As far as I can tell, all classes are too long if the standard is not having to attend at all, and any reading is too much reading.

For tenure-track faculty in particular, whose case for keeping their jobs rests in part on how their students rate them, it makes way more sense to be "nice" and easy than it does to be a drill sergeant. (To be fair, in my role as a member of the promotion and tenure committee, I have seen comments from students who express their appreciation for how much the instructor pushed them to do their best work.)

In short, assigning less work and giving high grades allows instructors more time for their own research or creative work, yields fewer complaints from disgruntled students, and results in higher numbers on the student evaluation forms. And so the dumbing down proceeds apace.

As for playing, I have the same thought whenever I see the games of whiffle-ball and touch football and horseshoes, the float-building for Homecoming, the rehearsals for Greek Sing: This isn't college. It's camp. When, I wonder, do they do their work?

Obviously, greater academic rigor alone won't put the kibosh on the destructive and inconsiderate behavior that often accompanies binge drinking. For one thing, no matter how much we pile on the work, they're still going to cut loose on Friday and Saturday nights. Indeed, increased weekday pressure might produce a concomitant amount of release on the weekends—a scary thought.

And we're still going to want the cops to patrol the streets and the courts to impose fines and the university to eject serial lawbreakers. And we still want the college experience to include Homecoming and Greek Sing and all that other fun stuff.

But if we're serious about reducing the student drinking problem, the best place to start is by getting students to take school more seriously.

Life, Liberty, and the Pursuit of Drunkenness

MARCH 4, 2011

As a community volunteer, I was a flop. For one thing, I forgot my phone, so even if I saw a State Patty's Day reveler committing the crime of the century, I couldn't do anything about it.

I also failed to hook up with a posse. I showed up at St. Paul's UMC at 2:00 P.M., checked in, got my map, and plunged back into the roaring streets all by my lonesome, feeling like the proverbial brown shoe in a roomful of a tuxedos.

I was not, I confess, feeling kindly disposed toward the Woo people just then, having spent the morning grading a particularly putrid batch of papers. Instead of "maintaining a friendly, pleasant, calming presence," as we were instructed to do, I found myself glaring at the little darlings.

When wished a happy State Patty's Day, I did not wish back. When proffered a high five, I kept my hands in my pockets. When I looked them in the eye, they looked away: I was all their professors and all their fathers rolled into one.

I tried to see things from the Woo point of view. Compared to the fall semester, with its football and homecoming and Halloween weekends, the first half of spring semester is a pretty tame affair, offering only clean-and-sober Dance Marathon. This winter's frigid weather had a further chilling effect, so to speak, on the party scene. I was feeling cooped up and ready to cut loose myself.

Above all, as with Mardi Gras in New Orleans or Carnival in Rio, there's something thrilling about the suspension of everyday decorum. In *The Electric Kool-Aid Acid Test*, Tom Wolfe wrote that one had to choose: you were either on the bus with Ken Kesey and the Merry Pranksters or you were off the bus. During a normal weekend you're either cutting loose at a party or straightening up on the streets. But on State Patty's Day, the boundary between party and streets is erased. The whole town is a party! Everyone is drunk and wearing hideous green costumes! Everyone is on the bus! What a hoot!

I followed the party west on College Avenue to Fraser, then back east on Beaver. The only time I felt uncomfortable was when I walked beneath balconies, half expecting to be showered with beer or worse. But I didn't see anything untoward until I returned home to fetch my phone, glanced out my kitchen window, and spied a kid relieving himself on the hedge across the street.

At least it was the hedge. Later, when the Highlands neighborhood listserv began heating up, I learned that one of my neighbors caught a kid peeing on his porch.

"I made the guy scrub the entire surface down," Noah Coleman informed us. "Several sheets of unused drywall and a roll of insulation is now ruined . . . The offender was clueless (drunk) enough to ask in-between his profuse apologies, what frat my house was and if I knew of any good parties tonight."

We Highlanders have heard that one before. To a drunk, every house is a frat house. Thus, the home invasion stories. Thus the belief that non-Woo people don't belong in the Woo people's neighborhood. "If you want to leech off the college community without experiencing our presence," one of them responded to a neighbor's Tweet, "then move to Bellefonte."

At 11:00 P.M., I made another circuit of downtown. I saw a kid fall flat on his face on College and another get cuffed on my street. Aside from a merry sing-along at the corner of College and Allen, I mostly saw kids who looked like they weren't having as much fun as they were supposed to be having. They wore the same disillusioned expressions as the little kid who nags his mom into putting a quarter in the slot of the horsey ride outside the supermarket, climbs on, and realizes how totally lame it is.

Of course, by then the party had been going for more than twelve hours. Drinkers tend to feel elated for a little while and deflated for a long while. And even apart from the body's finite capacity for alcohol, how many hours can you spend whooping and wandering from Frat Row to Beaver Canyon and back? The party was everywhere, which meant that ultimately, it was nowhere.

By the time it was over, the police had fielded almost five hundred calls, but the only really alarming totals were the number of drinkers who needed medical treatment (sixty-nine) and the number of DUI arrests (fourteen). Most of the arrests were for open containers, underage drinking, and public drunkenness. In short, State Patty's 2011 wasn't all that violent or destructive. It was just stupid.

In the streets of Tunis, Cairo, Manama, Tripoli, and Sana'a, masses of people are demanding civil liberties and social justice. In the streets of State College, the masses asserted their right to get wasted.

How inspiring.

Secrets of the Woo People Revealed

APRIL 22, 2011

You will give these instructions to no one. You will carry them with you at all times. You will maintain complete silence at all times unless told to speak. You will NOT use tobacco. You will NOT eat between meals. ONLY water is permitted as a beverage. You will sleep ONLY when told to do so.

These are among twenty-three commandments printed on one letter-sized sheet of white paper that was found on a local roadway. Preliminary examination of the document suggests it is a guide for young men who seek induction into the ranks of Sigma Chi, one of the secret societies of the Woo people, the nocturnal tribe that lives in sex-segregated longhouses, subsists on beverages concocted from fermented barley, and disks of dough slathered in crushed tomatoes and melted cheese, and pierces the nighttime silence with its warlike cries.

Anthropologists have long sought to study the myths and rituals of the Woo people. The problem has been that access to such arcana has been limited to the initiated. Scholars who had thought the Woo a band of savages may now have to revise their view in light of the strict observances enumerated in "Instructions for I-Period," as the document is titled.

In addition to the prohibitions against tobacco and snacking, novices, or pledges, as the Woo call them, must "maintain silence at all times unless told to speak by a brother." They must indicate their desire to speak by raising their right hand. They must spend their time in the dining room of the longhouse studying when not in class or "doing a duty."

Perhaps the harshest deprivation has to do with the glowing devices the Woo people use to remain in constant communication with their familiars at a distance: "You will have your phone off when you are in the house."

Pledges are, however, required to answer the house phone by the third ring "and recite the following memorized spiel": " . . . This is the domicile of the proud and worthy wearers of the white cross." The spiel continues with recitation of the founding myth of Sigma Chi and its "240 glorious chapters." The pledge then says, "I aspire to membership in that noble order. With whom do you wish to converse?"

The other mortifications of the flesh the pledges must undergo involve their sleep schedule and their daily journey to the houses of instruction: "You will be up, showered, shaved and at the house by 7:30 A.M. every morning . . . You are men of high ambition! There is no need to take the bus. WALK TO CLASS!"

During the indoctrination period, pledges are also expected to keep a diary "of all thoughts," write an autobiography, and carve a wax cross.

Perhaps the strangest ritual the recruits are required to enact occurs during their passage from one level of the longhouse to another: "You will go up and down the stairs to the first floor hallway, and the main stairs backwards using the railing."

Ethnographers are particularly intrigued by a hymn the pledges must sing while standing in front of the longhouse fireplace before the evening meal. The hymn is sung to "The Sweetheart of Sigma Chi," evidently a celestial goddess:

The blue of her eye and the gold of her hair
Are a blend of the western sky
And the moonlight beams on the girl of my dreams
She's the sweetheart of Sigma Chi.

Number twenty-three, the final item on the list, suggests that the preceding twenty-two rules governed the lives of pledges during their first week of initiation: a new set of rules for Week

Two was forthcoming. "Your journey has just begun," the document concludes.

Anthropologists love knowing the rules that govern a society; they are equally interested in knowing what happens to those who violate them. What, for example, became of the pledge—let's call him Siggy—who dropped the "Instructions for I-Period" on Shortlidge Road near the HUB parking deck? He was enjoined to give them to no one, to carry them at all times, and to "know them in detail." Assuming he hadn't yet memorized his marching orders, the only way he could avoid breaking any of the other taboos would be if he violated yet another one—the prohibition against speaking unless told to speak by a brother—by asking one of his co-pledges if he could copy his instructions.

Of course, it is also possible that Siggy decided that he did not like being told when to eat, speak, sleep, or worst of all, phone, and so discarded his instructions in disgust and no longer aspired to membership in that noble order. Maybe he had a crisis of belief in the Sweetheart of Sigma Chi or the wax cross.

If so, the anthropologists of the Woo people would love to debrief him. There is so much more they long to know about this mysterious people.

Let the Joyous News Be Spread

MAY 6, 2011

I heard the news about Osama bin Laden while watching the Mets-Phillies game last Sunday night. The fans at the ballpark began chanting "USA! USA!" Toggling between the game and the news while waiting for the president to speak, I saw that a crowd had gathered at the White House and that those people, too, had taken up the chant. It didn't occur to me that anyone in State College would do the same, but as I headed up to bed after watching President Obama make his announcement, I heard vuvuzelas and shouts coming from downtown.

I was surprised by all this because we so rarely celebrate death. I thought of the Munchkins singing "Ding Dong! The Witch is dead" and was struck, for the first time, by how odd that familiar song is.

Bin Laden, I realize, was our national bogeyman for the past ten years. He shadowed college-aged kids for much of their lives. How deeply has the fear of terrorism, and of bin Laden as the personification of that fear, worked its way into their psyches, I wonder?

In writing about Penn State's drinking problem on and off for the past couple of years, I've observed that there's a desperate edge to the party culture around here. Kids who drink themselves into unconsciousness, into the emergency room, or into the beds of strangers aren't just trying to have a good time. They're trying to obliterate themselves. Some of it, I'm sure, reflects the painful awkwardness of late adolescence. Some of it reflects their anxiety about how they're going to fare in the less-than-robust job market that awaits them when they get out of school. But beneath both those proximate causes lurks, perhaps, their sense that they are inheriting a dangerous world, a country beset by malevolent forces.

True, we of their parents' generation had The Bomb to worry about, which was more of a bogeyman than the leaders—Khrushchev, Brezhnev, Mao—who had it at their disposal (*Washington Post* cartoonist Herblock drew countless anthropomorphized versions of The Bomb). But as has often been pointed out, the difference between those earlier threats and the one posed by al-Qaeda is that this one actually came ashore. It wasn't hypothetical. It was real. It shook us. Our kids—these kids—suddenly found themselves in a children's book world where the grown-ups could not be counted on to keep them safe. They would have to fend for themselves.

And then our government's failure to hunt down bin Laden, to vanquish his real or imagined allies in Iraq and Afghanistan, along with its failure to respond effectively to Hurricane Katrina and the near-collapse of the economy, demoralized us. More than at most times in American history, we had a corrosive sense that our leaders—our symbolic parents—were not up to the great tasks of protecting us from harm and solving our problems.

America, you might say, has been depressed, in the clinical rather than the economic sense. If so, the best thing about the demise of Osama bin Laden may be that it restores confidence.

Remember when Jerry Ford, upon taking over for the disgraced Nixon, declared that "our long national nightmare is over?" Remember when Nixon himself, in justifying the 1970 incursion into Cambodia, warned that America would be "like a pitiful, helpless giant" if it failed to stand up to the North Vietnamese?

Maybe the spontaneous rallies in Beaver Canyon, in Times Square, at the White House, and at countless other locations around the country were an expression of just those hopes—that getting bin Laden, finally, signals an end to our latest long, national nightmare and quells, for now, those pitiful, helpless giant fears.

Such hopes may be dashed. They may even be groundless—the Ford presidency and the Cambodian incursion didn't turn out too well—but it's hard to overestimate the role of confidence in the lives of both individuals and societies. Wall Street analysts are forever talking about investor confidence. The slightest ripple of economic news can, on a mass scale, spur enormous numbers of people to buy or sell.

Might the news that the Wicked Witch of the East has gone where the goblins go boost confidence in President Obama (and boost President Obama's confidence in himself), stimulate investment, and in general lift the country out of a ten-year funk? Or, as the mayor of Munchkinland might put it, is this a day of independence for all the Munchkins and their descendants?

Too soon to say, obviously. A friend of mine was dismissive of the outpouring of joy in Beaver Canyon. Any excuse to party, he said. But I appreciated seeing the Munchkins sing and ring the bells out (or, in this case, blow the vuvuzelas) over something other than beating the Buckeyes.

Noise Essential to Woo Life, Researcher Says

SEPTEMBER 30, 2011

I have been asked, as a folklorist who has devoted the past fifteen years to studying the lifeways of the Woo people, what I think of State College's proposed noise ordinance.

I think it would be catastrophic.

The Woo people, after all, take their name from the noise they make. Deprive them of the right to raise a ruckus and we imperil their survival as a distinct people.

Like so many seemingly irrational behaviors that turn out, upon closer observation in the field, to serve a crucial culture-maintaining function, noisemaking plays a vital role in the social life of the Woo.

The Woo are in a late-adolescent life stage when interpersonal communication is extremely difficult and painfully awkward. The males, in particular, have only recently emerged from the grunting phase of their development when they arrive in Wooland. Playing loud music, especially while imbibing eloquence-impairing fermented beverages, neatly solves this problem by making all conversation, apart from the occasional "woo" cry, impossible.

The difficulty of interpersonal communication among the Woo has been exacerbated in recent times by the introduction of non-oral communication devices. Indeed, Woo couples frequently can be observed tapping furiously on these devices instead of talking to each other or even gazing soulfully into each other's eyes while sharing a meal at a public dining establishment.

Between the loud music that fills their nights and the incessant "texting" that dominates their days, oral communication skills might well be atrophying among the Woo. If so, proponents argue, noise restrictions could lead to a revival of such skills.

But the elders who instruct the Woo in the great halls of learning fear the situation is beyond remedy: they report indications that the ability to speak and listen has already gone by the wayside. If they are correct, the loud gatherings might be the only thing keeping the Woo people from total social disintegration.

The other reason not to enact a noise ordinance is that it could suppress Woo generosity. So transported are the Woo by the dulcet screams and gentle pounding of their favorite singers and instrumentalists that they wish to share their music with all who are fortunate enough to live within earshot. As is often the case in societies where gift exchanges are an important component of social life, refusing what is offered is simply out of the question.

Those who prefer moral suasion to legislative remedies ask whether the Woo might be prevailed upon to voluntarily restrict their music-sharing to the hours before midnight in deference to their non-Woo neighbors, most of whom are diurnal rather than nocturnal.

The problem there is that while the Woo gladly share their music with fellow tribesmen, they evince a selective blindness, often found in insular societies, toward outsiders. Consider, for example, how Javanese villagers responded to the arrival of anthropologist Clifford Geertz to study their culture:

"We were intruders, professional ones," Geertz wrote, "and the villagers dealt with us as Balinese seem always to deal with people not part of their lives who yet press themselves upon them: as though we were not there. For them . . . we were nonpersons, specters, invisible men.

" . . . People seemed to look right through us with a gaze focused several yards behind us on some more actual stone or tree. Almost nobody greeted us . . . they acted as if we simply did not exist."

A walk through the Highlands suggests that things are much the same with the Woo people. When informed of non-Woo complaints about their nocturnal activities, they often declare that non-Woo persons should not be living in Wooland, thereby ignoring the incontrovertible fact that many of the dwellings in their midst have been continuously occupied by non-Woo families for almost a century.

These, then, are delicate matters. My recommendation: rather than rush into a vote on a noise ordinance, the Borough Council should engage a team of ethnographic fieldworkers to conduct a cultural impact study. Such studies are modeled on the more familiar environmental impact report. The thinking is that just as any significant change in land use could profoundly affect the physical and spiritual resources of air, water, flora, fauna, land forms, and scenic values, it could also profoundly affect the humans who live in the region.

The Woo people have developed a way of life that centers on communal habitation wherein social solidarity is maintained through the ritual inducement of trance-like states via prolonged exposure to loud music and prolonged consumption of fermented beverages. Disruption of these rituals could disrupt the culture.

The result: the further diminution of human diversity, for which we all would be the poorer.

Before local government legislates this unique people out of existence, there needs to be dispassionate scientific investigation of the impact of noise restrictions on this fragile population.

Specifically, we need answers to such questions as: How much woo would a Woo person pitch if a Woo person couldn't pitch woo?

We Are—Going to Be OK

NOVEMBER 11, 2011

It's time to stop calling this place Happy Valley. The name doesn't fit. It never did.

The out-of-town reporters describe us as "an idyllic community," "a tranquil football Eden" "nestled" in the mountains of central Pennsylvania.

Spare us. As many Penn State students have learned this week, this is the real world, where the grown-ups in charge are craven, conniving, or clueless—and maybe all three. There are no saints here.

Joe Paterno made enormous contributions to this university. But he's not a cardboard cutout in a shop window. He's a man, with all the flaws that men have. It's touching that so many students thought otherwise. Now they know.

Now they know what a media circus looks like. Three students in my ethics class told me they saw reporters trying to incite the crowd that gathered in Beaver Canyon on Wednesday night. One raised and lowered his arms, the way football players do when they want the crowd to make more noise. One complained that what he was seeing wasn't a riot, and urged the students around him do better. One told the students he interviewed what he wanted them to say.

They got their riot. But here's the unfortunate thing. A thousand people can mill around peacefully for ninety-nine minutes, but if twenty-five people get violent or destructive for one minute, those images will lead the newscasts and make the front page.

One of my students was interviewed on one of those radio shows where the hosts abuse their guests for the amusement of their audience. She called the riot "an irrational response to rational anger."

You or I may agree or disagree about whether the Board of Trustees should or should not have let Paterno finish the season, but certainly a college student did not deserve to be ridiculed—and then made the target of hateful Tweets and Facebook postings—for articulating the view that Paterno deserved better than what he got.

She was the second of my students who cried on Thursday. Little wonder that in addition to chanting that Paterno be given "one more game," the students in Beaver Canyon late Wednesday cursed the news media.

As a journalism critic who is also a journalism advocate, I mounted a defense in my ethics class. True, lurid sex + celebrity + schadenfreude (ah, the pleasure of seeing the self-righteous laid low) make for an irresistible story, but would you rather have the news media do what Penn State administrators seem to have done and sweep a tale of child abuse under the rug? This was a story that needed to be told.

Not surprisingly, the students are also deeply worried about the reputation of the university and the devaluation of their degrees. One member of my class said that a company had rescinded its offer of an internship to her friend because it no longer wanted to take on a Penn State student.

This caused my urban legend antennae to go up, but even if the story is true, I told my class I would be very surprised if very many prospective employers would punish the students for the sins of their leaders.

Because when the satellite trucks roll out of town and the Queen-of-Hearts columnists stop screaming "Off with their heads," our reputation as a great university won't rest on our winning football tradition or our legendary football coach, but on our engaged and compassionate students and teachers and researchers.

One of my ethics students asked me how the faculty felt about the revelations and upheavals of the past week. I teased her about asking such a reporter's question. Some, I suspect, think Coach Paterno did what he was supposed to do and should have been allowed to retire when he was good and ready. Some probably think he didn't do nearly enough and should have been shown the door. And some, I'll wager, glanced up at the latest media freak show, shook their heads, and went back to their microscopes and data sets.

But here's what I think. Many of us pointy-headed PhDs don our Penn State sweatshirts and ball caps and gather in front of flat-screen TVs to eat pizza and watch the game, just like everyone else. But even among the most rabid fans are those who think our culture cares a little too much about sports and not enough about things that ought to matter more.

When I came out of my ethics class on Thursday, I ran into Dan Walden, founder of Penn State's American Studies, Jewish Studies, and African American Studies programs. He's been here as long as Joe Paterno and should be just as recognizable and just as beloved.

If any good can come out of this ghastly situation, apart from increasing awareness of child abuse, maybe, just maybe it will lead us all to restore the lost balance among academics, athletics, and partying.

We—the students, faculty, and staff—are Penn State. Not Graham Spanier. Certainly not Jerry Sandusky. Not even Joe Paterno.

Seeing Something and Saying Something

DECEMBER 15, 2011

In "The Last Picture Show," a 1971 movie that's stayed in my head for forty years, some bored high school boys amuse themselves by arranging the sexual initiation of their "slow" friend.

You can tell that one of the guys, the lead character played by Timothy Bottoms, knows in his bones that this is a cruel and sordid business, but he can't summon the courage to stand against the jokey machismo of his peers. He doesn't actively participate; he just watches, shame-faced.

When the boy's protector, Sam the Lion, sees what's happened, he (played by Ben Johnson) delivers one of the movie's great speeches: "You boys can get on out of here, I don't want to have no more to do with you. Scarin' a poor, unfortunate creature like Billy just so's you could have a few laughs—I've been around that trashy behavior all my life, I'm gettin' tired of puttin' up with it. Now you can stay out of this pool hall, out of my cafe, and my picture show too—I don't want no more of your business."

Haven't we all been around some kind of trashy behavior at one time or another, and failed to act or speak?

Of all the conversations I've had about the Sandusky scandal, the one that stays with me wrestled with just that question. We had been reading about what Mike McQueary says he saw and then did, and what Joe Paterno and Tim Curley and Gary Schultz and Graham Spanier said they heard and did, along with the comments of readers who were quite sure they would have pulled Sandusky off his victim and gone to the police and can't fathom why all these respected and, in the case of Paterno, revered figures didn't do the right thing.

We would all like to think we would unhesitatingly come to the aid of victims, but in trying to understand how or why these guys might have failed to act, my little group of friends tried to recall our own shameful failures of moral courage. One participant in this discussion remembered an experience quite similar to the "Last Picture Show" scenario I just sketched out. In this case the victim wasn't a developmentally disabled boy, but an injured bird. The bored teens thought it would be amusing to place the bird under the tire of a car, then rev the engine. Our friend was horrified at the cruelty of it, but could only watch, mutely.

You don't forget moments like that.

Someone else in the group remembered being called "a faggot," one of those situations where one is supposed to be a good sport about being teased when you actually feel humiliated. If I'm getting our friend's reaction right, the episode was doubly painful: he was both offended by the other person's homophobia and ashamed of his own.

His story brought back the many times when I've smiled weakly at a racist or anti-Semitic remark or joke, but said nothing. I also dimly remember abandoning my friend Arthur when he was teased about being fat. I was a chubby kid myself, and grateful to Arthur and his tormentors that they were teasing him rather than me. The vagueness of that recollection makes me suspect that there are other, worse ones, that I've blotted out altogether.

We can't undo such moments. But maybe we can atone for them by doing the right thing the next time. Just after the earthquake in Haiti two years ago, I was on a plane to Florida. When my seatmate asked me the reason for my visit, I told her my mom was in the hospital. She said she'd pray for her and talked about how, if my mother was suffering, it might be time for her to be "called home."

Not exactly how I see the world, but fine, the woman meant well. But then she started talking about all the Haitians she had encountered in the health care industry in south Florida, and how they were such hateful people, and that maybe the quake was God's punishment for their hatefulness.

The hatefulness of her own words was magnified by her piety. I couldn't let it pass. As politely as I could, I said the obvious thing:

that in my experience there were good and bad people in every group, that you couldn't generalize, etc.

That put an end to that conversation, which was a happy outcome. I was under no illusion that I had made her see the error of her ways. It wasn't about her. It was about my having seen the error of my own ways.

We are instructed, in the Age of Terrorism, that if we see something, we should say something. That should apply to the local acts of terrorism—the trashy behavior—we see in our everyday lives as well.

We've Got to Get Ourselves Back to the Garden

FEBRUARY 3, 2012

At first glance, we, the faculty of the Pennsylvania State University, appear to be sorely negligent in the performance of our duties.

As befits an institution that was originally called the Farmers' High School (1855) and whose name was later changed to the Agricultural College of Pennsylvania (1862), our charter calls for the "instruction of youth in the art of farming."

In fact, our bucolic campus (Latin for "field") was chosen, in part, for its serviceability as a farm, to be worked by the "pupils [who] shall thus be instructed and taught all things necessary to be known by a farmer."

This commitment to agriculture education, by the way, is why six of the thirty-two trustees charged with governing an institution of higher learning are supposed to represent "organized agricultural societies or organizations."

(Keith Masser, the board's new vice chairman, is one of the six. In 2005 he was named the Vance Publishing Potato Man of the Year, a title to which very few of us could lay claim. With Masser as veep and Karen Peetz as the new chair, should we henceforth refer to board of trustees meetings as Masser-Peetz Theatre?)

Notwithstanding this clear ag-ed orientation, very few of us faculty types know beans about farming. Where I come from, for example, dairy was a meatless meal. A spread was something you put on a bagel. Ranch was a salad dressing. The Garden was where the Knicks played. Barns were what wild pitchers couldn't hit the broad side of. A bushel and a peck measured degrees of romantic attachment.

A city slicker like me is supposed to instruct youth in the art of farming?

Well, if we read further into the charter, we see that the university's founders held a laudably expansive idea of what kinds of expertise the faculty should have: "a knowledge of the English language, grammar, geography, history, mathematics, chemistry, and such other branches of natural and exact science as will conduce to the proper education of a farmer."

Heck, I teach knowledge of the English language and grammar. And journalism is often said to be the first rough draft of history. What's more, our journalism classes are aggier than they might at first appear. Students who take them learn how to cultivate sources, rake muck, and separate the wheat from the chaff, all of which prepares them to produce journalism worthy of a Pullet Surprise.

Still, we could do more. I think of an interview I did with an Italian-American guy who took me on a tour of his garden. "Italians hate a lawn," he declared. "We don't grow anything we can't eat."

Think of how much lawn can be turned to ag-educational use here at University Park. Every college or department could have its own plot. The English Department could plant a Shakespeare garden. The historians could grow heirloom vegetables. The anthropologists could use their knowledge of ethnobotany to raise medicinal plants.

Business majors could open a petting zoo featuring bulls and bears. Or, if the Smeal College of Business wanted to collaborate with the College of Communications and the political science department, the menagerie could include hawks, doves, donkeys, elephants, lame ducks, watchdogs, paper tigers, and pigs, provided they wear lipstick.

Meanwhile, at the residence halls, the students could sow their wild oats. What, they're already doing that? So much the better!

Alternatively, we could keep the campus the way it is and change the university's charter and bylaws. After all, they've been changed before, lots of times. Everything from the name of the institution (Pennsylvania State College in 1874, Pennsylvania State University in 1953) to the number of trustees (thirty-two to twenty-three to thirty-two to thirty-one to thirty-two), to the way in which the trustees are chosen.

Some people think thirty-two trustees is too darned many and would like to see a more streamlined board.

Some think agriculture is now overrepresented on the board, given how much the Farmers' High School has grown beyond its aggie roots.

Some wonder why the composition of the board of trustees privileges business and agriculture over other fields of endeavor, such as the arts, the humanities, and the social sciences. And what qualifies corporate types to call the shots at an institution of higher learning, anyway? You don't see too many academics on the boards of the corporations, do you?

Finally, some wonder whether it's a conflict of interest for the governor of the commonwealth to serve on the board of trustees, given that the governor is often trying to minimize the state's appropriation to the university while the board of trustees should be trying to maximize the state's appropriation to the university.

Ah, but guess who has the power to amend the charter and bylaws of the university. Yep, the board of trustees.

Now where's my muck rake?

So Many Opinions, So Few Facts

FEBRUARY 10, 2012

Liberals are godless commies! Conservatives are heartless bigots! Digital technology is bringing us together as never before! Digital technology is isolating us as never before! Derek Jeter is overrated! Derek Jeter is an all-time great!

Opinions, it is said, are like, um, certain bodily portals: everyone has one. And more and more, everyone feels free to stick theirs right in your face. Yuk.

"IMHO," indeed. If there's one thing people are not humble about these days, it's their opinions.

Take the Sandusky scandal. Even now, three months after the filing of the charges and the release of the Grand Jury report, there is so much we do not know about what was seen, heard, and done. And we may never know. Much of it may not even be knowable.

According to a recent story in the *New York Times*, the more we study memory, the less reliable memory turns out to be: "Hundreds of studies have catalogued a long list of circumstances that can affect how memories are recorded and replayed, including the emotion at the time of the event, the social pressures that taint its reconstruction, even flourishes unknowingly added after the fact."

The *Times* story didn't mention the Sandusky scandal, which had hit the news just a few weeks prior. But I couldn't help thinking of the emotions and social pressures that may have tainted the memories of the men who were involved in the conversations about what Mike McQueary witnessed in the showers ten years ago.

McQueary's testimony is a small part of the case against Jerry Sandusky—there's the testimony of all those alleged victims, after all—but it is a huge part of the legal case against Tim Curley and Gary Schultz, as well as the moral case against Joe Paterno and Graham Spanier. And here, memories, and possibly motives, differ.

McQueary has testified that he's pretty sure he saw Jerry Sandusky having sexual intercourse with a boy, but that he could not bring himself to be that explicit with Paterno. That accords with Paterno's testimony: he said McQueary told him he saw Sandusky "fondling or doing something of a sexual nature."

According to his testimony at the preliminary hearing of the charges against Curley and Schultz in December, McQueary went into a bit more detail when he met with the two administrators: he described what he saw as "extremely sexual" and indicated that "some kind of intercourse was going on."

But that's not what Curley and Schultz said they heard. Curley recalled "inappropriate conduct" and "horsing around." Schultz recalled the grabbing of genitals while wrestling, which he characterized as "not that serious . . . no indication that a crime had occurred." Both deny being told anything about intercourse.

If McQueary is remembering correctly and truthfully, then there's no excuse for Curley and Schultz (and possibly Spanier) not having gone to the police.

If Curley and Schultz are remembering correctly and truthfully, we might be able to see how, not wanting to destroy Sandusky or get the university embroiled in an ugly scandal, they would hope it would be enough to tell Sandusky to quit "horsing around" with kids in ways that could be misinterpreted. But Schultz, at least, is still on the hook for having known about the 1998 investigation. So are Paterno and McQueary, with their greater appreciation of the "seriousness" of the misconduct, for not having followed up—as Paterno himself acknowledged.

Bottom line, we don't know who is remembering correctly and truthfully. Maybe McQueary was so uncomfortable with his role that he watered down his account to a degree that allowed Curley and Schultz to categorize Sandusky's behavior as horseplay, which would have been how they preferred to look at it. Maybe McQueary has talked himself into remembering that he was more frank than he actually was. Maybe Curley and Schultz are guilty as charged.

Has all this uncertainty stopped anyone from weighing in on the guilt or innocence of the various parties? Heck, no. In this cultural moment, one must stake out a position and defend it against all comers. To say, "Well, let's wait and see," or, "You know, this is a complicated issue," is to lack a moral compass.

It wouldn't matter so much if the bomb throwing only took place in the comments section appended to every online news story. Let the vox populi ring out. But the indifference to facts, and the unwillingness to grant legitimacy to anyone who disagrees with us seems to have spilled over into and suffused our politics, which more and more resembles a demolition derby.

Forget compromise. Forget seeing the world from the other guy's point of view. Forget the possibility that we may be wrong, that we may not know all the facts.

We don't discuss anymore. We flame.

THON (Jekyll) vs. State Patty's (Hyde)

FEBRUARY 17, 2012

It's Jekyll-and-Hyde time here in the land formerly known as Happy Valley.

This week, the Penn State IFC/Panhellenic Dance Marathon (Jekyll).

Next week, State Patty's Day (Hyde).

This weekend, Penn State students will counter the football-loving-louts image that dominated the airwaves after Joe Paterno was sacked by announcing that they've once again raised millions to help children with pediatric cancer and their families. The sanctimony that drips from this event can be a bit Jekyll-like, but still: bravo, bravo, bravo.

Next weekend, Penn State students are scheduled to reinforce the F-L-L image by painting the town green. Many of us killjoys are still hoping against hope that this year's edition of State Patty's Day will be a bust.

Everyone knows that none of the State Patty's celebrations have made any sense since the first one in 2007. That year, freakishly, St. Patrick's Day and spring break overlapped. State Patty's Day was a playful way for Penn State students to have the party here, together, before they dispersed for the weeklong breather. Almost heartwarming, really.

This year, like all the years since 2007, spring break *precedes* St. Paddy's day; ergo, no need for the State version. Of course, the same could have been said in the years 2008–11, and the green beer flowed anyway.

But as many commentators have pointed out, this year is different. Our reputation has been damaged. Yes, some of the criticism has been unfair: Not everyone protested Paterno's firing. Not everyone who protested Paterno's firing rioted.

There's more at stake than damage to reputation, though. A rottenness in the culture has been exposed. The rottenness isn't football and it isn't drinking. It's too much football and too much drinking—a matter of skewed priorities.

These pastimes, as pleasurable as they may be, should not be why anyone enrolls here. (No disrespect to Coach Paterno, but those who said he was the reason they came to Penn State need to find a better reason.) A meager turnout for State Patty's Day would signal that the students get that.

Needless to say, preachments from faculty members like me or Laurie Mulvey and Sam Richards, community members, Penn State administrators, or even student leaders won't have any impact. Our young scholars will have to decide for themselves whether they want to participate in this travesty of a tradition.

Again, this isn't just about how it's going to look on YouTube, or whether "The Daily Show," "South Park," and "Saturday Night Live" are going to pick on us again. It's about growing up a little, becoming a little more, shall we say, temperate.

I was originally going to say "serious" rather than "temperate," but as the last few months have shown, life's grim enough. I'm for as much silliness as we can get away with.

Paterno's death only deepened the pall cast by the Sandusky scandal. A month after his death, the gloom lingers. So I can see how the students might be particularly eager to cut loose. I can also see how they might want to thumb their noses at the finger waggers who don't want them to cut loose.

I just think it would be best for all concerned if they could hang in there for one more week and cut loose someplace else. After all, isn't that what spring break is for?

Thinking about Dr. Jekyll and Mr. Hyde prompted me to go back to Stevenson's story. Jekyll's account of how he felt at the moment he imbibed the potion that would turn him into Mr. Hyde reads like a pretty apt description of what happens when one is on a binge:

"There was something strange in my sensations, something indescribably new and, from its very novelty, incredibly sweet. I felt younger, lighter, happier in body; within I was conscious of a heady recklessness, a current of disordered sensual images running like a mill-race in my fancy, a solution of the bonds of obligation, an unknown but not an innocent freedom of the soul. I knew myself, at the first breath of this new life, to be more wicked, tenfold more wicked, sold a slave to my original evil; and the thought, in that moment, braced and delighted me like wine. I stretched out my hands, exulting in the freshness of these sensations."

It's not the drinking that's the problem. It's the wickedness. Quaint word, I know. But there's nothing quaint about vandalism or assaults.

Defenders of State Patty's Day think their freedom to have drinks with friends is under attack. It's not, though. It's destructive drinking that we all worry about, the kind that causes people to hurt themselves and to hurt others.

The kind that turns the Dr. Jekylls of THON into the Mr. Hydes of State Patty's Day.

The Fumbler and the Furnisher

APRIL 20, 2012

If you are shopping for a house in the borough of State College, please do not read the following story.

Late last Saturday afternoon—hey, no peeking!—three young men came galloping across my front lawn. One carried a football. The other two were trying to relieve him of it.

The one with the ball stumbled or maybe was shoved into a tree. He fumbled the ball, bounced off the tree, tripped over the curb, and fell on his face in the street.

The other two guys, naturally, rushed over to see if he was OK.

Just kidding. The other two guys, having recovered the fumble, ran, laughing, back up the street. I called 911.

A moment later, still laid out, eyes closed, cartoon birdies circling his head, practically, the stumbler-turned-fumbler turned mumbler—a good sign under the circumstances. Mostly, he was colorfully swearing that he was not going to sue someone or other.

Since I couldn't get him to get up and get out of harm's way, I assumed the role of traffic cop, waving cars around him. Soon, a young woman stopped to help. Then a neighbor came over. They pulled him to his feet and then forced him back down onto the grass when he tried to stagger away. Apart from a cut on his nose, he didn't look as bad as he surely felt.

Soon, a police car arrived, then an ambulance. The fumbler was not happy about the EMTs' ministrations but was way too wobbly to do anything about it. For a while he sounded like a scratched phonograph record, saying, "I'm not gonna (effing) . . . " over and over.

A few times he was able to advance the needle to "sue you" before he jumped back to "I'm not gonna."

The officer got the fumbler to divulge his name and birth date—yep, underage—and asked him if he'd been drinking. "Is the Pope Catholic?" I muttered.

The EMTs got him strapped to a backboard and explained to him that they were bringing him to the hospital to have his shoulder looked at.

And off everyone went.

The shocking part of this story, of course—aside from the fumbler's failure to appreciate that his face plant was not part of the marketing plan for my house—is his abandonment by his erstwhile companions. The obvious explanation is that they too were underage. In those situations, apparently, it's every man for himself. I have heard stories, for example, of underage drinkers driving an unconscious buddy to the emergency room and dumping him out and speeding off before anyone could question them.

Then there was the former student who popped into my office and began his tale of woe by saying, "I am in so much trouble."

The trouble started when a neighbor, too young to obtain a keg of beer for an upcoming bash, asked if he would be so kind. He agreed.

The furnisher didn't actually attend the party, but it must have been a good one—so good, that one ecstatic guest began jumping up and down on the sofa. The sofa, alas, was positioned rather close to a window. Thus, after one of his jumps, instead of landing back on the sofa, Bouncy Boy pitched out the window.

The distance from window to ground, according to the furnisher, was thirty-five feet. When the party hosts saw what had happened, they sprang into action. Specifically, they spent the next forty-five minutes cleaning the apartment.

Satisfied that one could no longer tell that this had been the scene of a jump-up-and-down-on-the-sofa kind of soiree, they called 911.

Bouncy Boy, who could not have spent a very enjoyable forty-five minutes in the bushes thirty-five feet below, turned out to have broken his back.

A critical component of the apartment cleanup, meanwhile, had been getting rid of the keg. The furnisher was thus summoned. Apprised of the situation, he did what any panicky twenty-one-year-old would have done: he loaded the keg onto his truck, drove into the woods, and cast the keg into the wilderness, never to be seen until later that night when the police, having traced keg to furnisher, persuaded him to show them where he had dumped it.

Unlike the non-litigious fumbler, the insurance company that paid the cost of putting Bouncy Boy together again sued the furnisher.

And that is why, like he said, he was in so much trouble.

The only good news in all this is that no one was touring my house at the time of the face-plant incident. But if any of you potential buyers ignored my suggestion that you skip this column, look at it this way: Life is about having stories to tell. Here in the Highlands, we've got a million of 'em.

Farewell to the Woo People

Today, I concede defeat. The Woo people have won. By the end of the month I will withdraw from the Woolands with all my chattels.

This was a war fought not with guns and steel, but with red plastic cups and loud music and wild cries in the night. I countered with righteous indignation. It was not enough. While I got grayer and balder and crankier, the Woo people drew on an inexhaustible supply of fresh recruits, cheap booze, and hyper-caffeinated beverages.

Still, I am proud to say that I withstood their onslaughts for sixteen years. Indulge, if you will, an old campaigner's nostalgia for the battles of yesteryear:

The Commandeered Corolla (1997)—On Halloween night, a band of Woo tribesmen tried the door to my station wagon, found it unlocked, released the parking brake, put the manual tranny in neutral, and rolled the car down the driveway and across the street, where I found it, undamaged, on All Saints Day, rear wheels on the grass, front wheels in the street, driver's side door open.

The Sack of the Porch Furniture (1998)—I stepped out my back door to take the morning air, and groggily thought the porch looked unusually tidy. A raiding party had come in the night and whisked away the table and chairs.

The False Peace Offering (c. 1995–2000)—A delegation of Woo warriors rang our bell one autumn afternoon to request permission to gather the leaves in our front yard for the purpose of re-scattering them on the dance floor inside their lodge house for an evening festival. We granted permission, then endured one of the Woo people's more protracted sonic assaults.

The Assault on the Flower Bed (c. 2000–2005)—On another morning I discovered the removable door from an SUV nestled among the azalea bushes in my front yard.

The Occupation of the Driveway (2010)—The tribal elders of the Woo people were in town that night. One of them daringly blockaded my driveway with his car. I called in reinforcements in the form of the local constabulary, who summoned a tow truck. Watching the removal of the offending vehicle—and the Woo daddy's attempt to talk his way out of it—was a satisfying spectacle.

The Panty Raid (2011)—This was a weak psych-ops attempt to distract or taunt the troops by festooning a perimeter plum tree with a thong.

Pretty tame stuff, all in all. Some of our allies endured worse, notably home invasions, where a besotted Woo tribesman stumbles into an unlocked house and passes out on a sofa or in a guest bedroom. Neighbors down the street were rudely awakened by a hammer crashing through their bedroom window.

But don't feel sorry for, or question the sanity of, the people who have bought my house. Thanks, in part, to what appeared to be my best efforts to sabotage any sale by describing life in the neighborhood in my columns, they're moving in eyes wide open, just as I did sixteen years ago. I'm a journalist, after all. You think I bought a house in the Woolands without walking the neighborhood and asking everyone I met what it was like to live so close to all those Woo lodge houses?

The verdict: yeah, it gets loud sometimes, but there are so many other nice things about the neighborhood that it's worth it.

I found that to be true. When I think about my time in the Woolands, I think less about the revelry than about reading bedtime stories to my children and playing whiffle-ball with them in the backyard.

I also appreciated commuting by bicycle or on foot to my job of lulling the Woo people to sleep after their nighttime frolics. I might have driven to work three times in all those years. I'll miss that.

I'll also miss my neighbors, who were an extraordinarily tolerant and neighborly bunch. After all, you have to be, to live among the Woo people.

In short, my departure from the Woolands has less to do with Woo people fatigue than four-bedroom house fatigue. With my youngest child graduating from high school this spring, I'm ready for a smaller house—and a smaller yard.

But first, Ukraine. I know it looks like I'm trying to get as far away from the Woo people as possible, but if that was my goal, I would have arranged to spend my sabbatical in Perth, Australia. And if all I was trying to do was escape the late-night howls of the Woo people, Boalsburg would have sufficed.

That said, I do not intend to return to the Woolands at the conclusion of my year away from Penn State. After sixteen years of close-range observation, I'm pretty sure I have gathered enough material to write my ethnography of this mysterious people.

Things are Just Peachy Around Here

JULY 20, 2012

It never ceases to amaze me: we could be on the brink of economic or ecological catastrophe, our roads and bridges crumbling to dust, our coastal cities threatened by surging seas, and we'll get worked up about flag burning or same-sex marriage, or this president's philandering and that one's birth certificate.

The latest instance: Penn State knowingly harbored a child rapist for at least a decade. So what are we arguing about? Changing the name of an ice cream flavor! Pulling down the Paterno statue! Suspending the football program!

All of these debates are a bit off the point. Yes, the honors we bestow reveal a lot about who and what we value. But passionate arguments over Peachy Paterno? Please.

And as for the statue, Joe Paterno has already been pulled down. What remains is a chunk of metal.

The hottest debate centers on the future of football. At issue is whether the Sandusky scandal is a football scandal. The commentators who seek the "death penalty" for Penn State football say of course it's a football scandal: The football coach was more powerful than anyone else at the university. When Joe Paterno said let's not call the law on Jerry Sandusky, the law was not called.

If that doesn't indicate a lack of "institutional control," to use the NCAA's term, what does?

I don't disagree. But I question whether there's any more "institutional control" at Michigan State, Ohio State, Boise State, or any other school with big-time athletic programs.

Ohio State President Gordon Gee's response to questions about whether he would fire Jim Tressel has been oft-quoted of late: "I'm just hopeful the coach doesn't dismiss me."

A revealing joke, if ever there was one. The importance of inter-collegiate sports is inflated to a preposterous degree. The Sandusky scandal is just further proof.

Instead of punishing Penn State football—its players, its new coaches, right down to the chambermaids who owe their jobs to the influx of out-of-towners on football weekends—we should all take a hard look at how we spend our time, our money, and our passion. The priorities are seriously awry.

Having agreed that the global culture of sports is pretty messed up, I also want to make a qualified defense of the local culture of Happy Valley (a nickname that will never again be used unironically).

Is there a cult of St. JoePa here? There is. A see-no-evil, circle-the-wagons mentality among true-blue members of Nittany Nation? No question.

The cult of JoePa offers further evidence that facts rarely change beliefs. If your starting point is faith that Paterno wouldn't do the things he is said to have done, then he simply couldn't have done them.

But every dominant culture spawns countercultures. In State College, the countercultures are arty, punky, folky, outdoorsy, intellectual, and political.

A couple of years ago, I was at a party attended by a number of international faculty members. There was talk of seeing some obscure movie at the State Theatre that Sunday night. Someone asked if they ought to get there early, in case there's a crowd.

I laughed. "Trust me," I said, "there is not going to be a crowd."

It was Super Bowl Sunday.

Clearly, not everyone around here lives and dies with what happens on green fields or hardwood courts. This place is more complicated than the "Mayberry" stereotypes we've seen in the national media. It's a college town, for crying out loud. Our faculty members come from all over the world and have been all over the world, which kind of gives the lie to views of the culture as insular.

But really, any small town has more layers than the metro dailies are able to make out from their urban perches. I know. I've lived in a few.

This is not an apology for Happy Valley. The Freeh report contains a host of recommendations aimed at preventing future abuses. It's not enough to say that Joe Paterno's longevity, success, and reputation for probity were unique and that neither new coach Bill O'Brien nor any of his successors will be able to amass that kind of power.

Nor is it enough to say that no future Penn State Board of Trustees will cede as much power to any future Penn State president as the old board ceded to Graham Spanier.

It is the job of everyone who cares about this university—trustees, administration, faculty, staff, students, and alumni—to see to it that effective checks and balances are installed, and to recommit to the idea of Penn State as a place where academics matter more than athletics.

These tasks are going to be a lot harder and more complicated than renaming an ice cream flavor, pulling down a statue, or finding something else to do on an autumn Saturday.

As I Was Saying . . .

JUNE 4, 2014

Allow me to reintroduce myself. Since I last wrote for StateCollege.com two summers ago I have:

- fomented a civil war in Ukraine;
- married the woman of my dreams (between the two of us we have five children in their twenties);
- moved four times, with a fifth coming next month;
- been orphaned by the death of my ninety-six-year-old papa;
- sent my baby boy off to college and watched my girls run marathons;
- driven from East Coast to West Coast and back again. (My advice: stay in the college towns—they have better restaurants.)

OK, I didn't actually stir up trouble in Ukraine. But things were calm when I got there and have been calamitous since I left, so my Penn State colleagues are blaming me.

In fact, I spent my time in Ukraine the way every stranger spends time in a strange land: trying to understand and be understood. It was a challenge. It was also refreshing, after a year of all Sandusky, all the time, to go someplace where no one had heard of Jerry, JoePa, or intercollegiate sporting events that draw one hundred thousand spectators.

I could write a book about my time in Ukraine, but for now I'll leave it at this: after observing its October 2012 parliamentary elections, I was not surprised that this long-troubled land began to unravel.

In the eastern part of the country, the ruling party of now-deposed Kleptocrat-in-Chief Viktor Yanukovych received 65 percent of the vote. In the West, where I was, his party captured less than 5 percent of the vote.

In the East, the ultranationalist Svoboda Party picked up slightly more than 1 percent of the vote. In the West, Svoboda led with 38 percent of the vote.

Those are some stark divisions. And now there are the imperial ambitions of Vladimir Putin, who might be mad. Loved ones tell me they're glad I left before Ukraine became a hot spot, but as one who still calls himself a journalist, I wish I were there, bearing witness.

The standard question when you return from a sabbatical is, how does it feel to be back? The expected answer is that it feels none too great: Back to the rat race. Back on the treadmill. Back to the daily grind.

Work needs a new publicist.

I was thrilled to get out from under the toxic Sandusky cloud for a year, but I was also happy to return. Here are four reasons:

1. The Joys of Gainful Employment—During my year away, I spent time with three friends who, like me, are at least halfway to one hundred. None of them has a steady income at the moment. I'm not just glad I have a tenured faculty job at this fine university. I'm glad I have any job whatsoever.

2. The Joys of Being Busy—I am getting close enough to retirement age to see a sabbatical as a preview. My conclusion: not ready. Retirees extol the joys of not having to be anywhere at any particular time, but I still like the routines of work. I like having places I need to go and things I need to do. I also like the culture of work: the doorway/hallway chats with colleagues, the chance meetings with students around campus. As much as people complain about their jobs, I think a lot of them like those things about work also. It's just not cool to admit it.

3. The Joys of No Longer Living Among the Woo People—I enjoyed my sixteen years in the frat zone, but I hold a higher opinion of Penn State students now that I'm not encountering

them at their loudest and most loutish. The tranquility of life on the other side of town ain't bad either.

4. The Joys of Campus Life—A snapshot from last fall: The lower half of the mall from Allen Street to Pattee Library is lined with blue balloons touting the Blue-and-White Bash. The upper half is lined with yellow balloons touting a marathon reading of Gabriel Garcia Marquez's *One Hundred Years of Solitude.*

After lending my voice to the Marquez marathon for five minutes, I head to a meeting of Penn State employees incensed about proposed changes to our health benefits that seem unduly invasive of our privacy. En route I bump into a former student who wants to talk about news coverage of a student who tweeted a racist complaint about noise in the HUB.

All of it, the Bash, the Marquezathon, the uproar over the healthcare initiative, and the uproar over the racist tweet, reminded me of what I love about campus life—not that it is a quiet island of peace and harmony—but that it is a noisy arena of struggle and conflict where people are trying to figure out what's right, what's fair, what's meaningful.

Some weeks this column will be a quiet island. Some weeks it will be a noisy arena.

Maybe some weeks it'll be both.

Greetings from Zombie Nation!

Among the results of the Penn State Values and Culture Survey that were made public last week was a finding that 85 percent of respondents either strongly agreed (52 percent) or agreed (33 percent) that they were proud to be members of the Penn State community.

That's an impressive number, but what does it mean? What is everyone so proud of?

This, the survey did not probe. It's enough that we all want to slosh around in this nice warm bath of Penn State Pride together.

It's similarly impossible to decipher the meaning of Penn State Pride from the comments of students and alumni who were interviewed for one of the many Homecoming stories that appeared in local news media last week. Some examples:

According to one attendee, the purpose of the carnival on the Old Main lawn—inflatable hamster ball, mechanical bull, etc.—was to "celebrate our Penn State pride."

An alumnus at the Homecoming Parade said, "I'm very proud of this school. I'm very proud to be a part of it."

An alumna at the Homecoming game, who cries when the drum major takes the field, described "an overwhelming sense of family and pride." Her daughter said the sense of pride had been evident all over campus during Homecoming Week.

That last comment, in particular, cries out for a follow-up question: Evident? How? What did you see, aside from T-shirts? What did you hear, aside from "We Are . . . Penn State!"?

Not to go all academic jargon on you, but scholars who are interested in how we use language might regard this thing called Penn

State Pride as a floating (or empty) signifier: it's not attached to anything in particular.

At this point I'm sure some of you readers are muttering, maybe even sputtering, that Frank just doesn't get it. Penn State Pride is a rich complex of feelings. It can't be put into words.

Maybe not. I'd like to see us try, though. We're a university, after all—a place devoted to questioning, examining, analyzing. Those who want to believe (or in the O'Brien "era," to "Billieve") should join a cult.

As near as I can figure, there are two kinds of pride. One is pride of identification or association: I'm proud to say I was born in Brooklyn simply because Brooklyn is cool (or was cool—its coolness seems to be fading).

When out-of-town guests admire the beauty of the Penn State campus, I feel proud of the place though I've not planted a single tree or designed a single building. I also feel proud to work at the same university as some of my brilliant colleagues.

Notice that I deserve no credit for any of these things.

The second kind of pride is connected to our own achievements: I'm proud when I do something good, like write something worth reading (some of you are probably saying, "Give it up, dude"), or when I stop procrastinating and do something I find difficult, like complete an application for financial aid or fix a leaky sink.

There's a lot to be said for the first kind of pride. It's communal, insofar as it connects me to my fellow Brooklynites. It's generous, insofar as it appreciates the contributions of my coworkers. It's custodial, insofar as it makes me less likely to litter and more inclined to pick up someone else's litter.

Above all, the second kind of pride should not be a precondition for the first kind: only the strictest Puritan would say that I have no right to feel proud of myself unless I do something to be proud of. Indeed, I probably have to feel proud of who I am to have the confidence to do the hard stuff that leads to my feeling proud of what I've done.

That said, there's something inane, not to mention immodest about all the quacking about Penn State Pride that goes on around here.

A wise friend of mine believes that the qualities we tout about ourselves are qualities that we actually lack. I'm inclined to agree. When, some years back, the leaders of Penn State's Black Caucus received racist death threats, buttons sprouted on lapels that said, "No Hate at Penn State," which meant, of course, that there was hate at Penn State.

Consider, in that light, the comments of a student at the Northwestern game who told a reporter that Penn State's pride has only grown stronger since the Sandusky scandal. "Nothing has changed," he said. "Things are back to normal."

Perhaps he's ashamed. And he doesn't want to feel like he has anything to be ashamed of. That's why the easing of the NCAA sanctions felt like an absolution.

But another wise friend thinks being absolved of blame for the Sandusky scandal does not absolve us of responsibility. We may not be to blame for what happened in the past, but we're all responsible for what happens in the future. Perhaps we have learned, for example, that if we are ever in the position that Spanier, Curley, Schultz, and Paterno were in, we can't just hope the problem goes away. We have to do the right thing, however uncomfortable doing the right thing might be.

That would be something to be proud of.

Putting it another way, we should be proud of what we contribute to Penn State, not just that We Are Penn State.

Welcome to Alt-State College!

OCTOBER 22, 2014

When the out-of-town reporters streamed in three years ago to cover the Sandusky case, they fed the facts—sordid crimes committed in a place that calls itself Happy Valley!—into their story-processing machines and out came the most glorious drivel.

How, the scribes asked, could such a "bucolic" or "idyllic" place (take your pick), "nestled" as it is in the mountains of Central Pennsylvania, be the scene of such foul deeds?

Here was my favorite scene-setter, published in the *Philadelphia Inquirer*, which ought to have known better: "The streets of State College are pristine, and the air there feels as if it has gone through some kind of natural filter . . . On a clear day, a sun-splashed day, with the Nittany Mountains on the horizon, the place seems as if it's been touched by the hand of God . . . Open your window in State College, you hear only the sweet sounds—sparrow tweets and cricket chirps."

Pristine streets, eh? Maybe the red maple leaves that still lay on the ground in early November camouflaged the red plastic beer cups.

Clear day? Yeah, we have some, but this is the cloudiest place I've ever lived.

Nittany Mountains? Uh, no such range.

Sweet sounds? The Woo people must have been sleeping.

OK, so that's how the city slickers see us. Sounds like they ought to get out of town more often. What's surprising is the extent to which we, who live here, buy into the Happy Valley image, including those of us who want no part of it.

Consider my composite friend, Professor Prig. Prig was destined for great things. He had to pay his dues, of course, so he accepted a position at this remote outpost of higher education, fully expecting his brilliant scholarly output to attract the attention of urban schools in New York, Boston, or Philadelphia, much as a baseball phenom expects a quick call-up to the major leagues after a dazzling stint in the minors.

In the meantime, he bemoans the paucity of decent restaurants and movie offerings and sneers at the lowbrow enthusiasms of the sports-crazed rabble. Oh, he's been to a tailgate, a football game, a Homecoming Parade, a Dance Marathon a time or two (he thought of it as research). But a little of that sort of thing goes a long way, don't you know?

With every passing year, Prig worries that his stint in the hinterlands is becoming a permanent banishment from the world's hippest places. If only, he says. If only there were more bookstores here, more coffeehouses, more jazz clubs, more galleries, more ethnic restaurants, fewer pizza joints, fewer T-shirt shops, fewer student hangouts, fewer drunks.

The good professor doesn't dislike Happy Valley. Far from it. He likes it as a low-overhead base of operations that enables him to travel more than he could if he were living in the big city. But the idea is to get out of here as often as possible for as long as possible (thank heavens for academic conferences).

Were Prig to stick around a little, he might see that there's more here than meets the eye. Call it Alt-State College. It's not any particular group of people, but a dimension of mind, like the Twilight Zone. Alt-State College is the sum of all the little subcultures that coexist alongside the town's high-profile sports and drinking culture.

It's the folkies you see at the Acoustic Brew concerts; the film and drama buffs you see at the State Theatre, the Downtown Theatre Centre, and on campus; and the literature lovers you see at readings at Webster's and on campus.

Alt-State College is the hikers you meet in the Rothrock State Forest, the cyclists active in the Centre Region Bike Coalition, and the farmers and locavores involved in Community Supported Agriculture.

Increasingly, Alt-State College is the international students and faculty members and their families whose presence gives the lie to those portrayals of Happy Valley as an insular or provincial backwater.

The above groups are a top-of-the-head list. I'm sure there are many I don't even know about. Also, there are no boundaries separating the dominant culture from the subcultures. Plenty of poetry lovers, for example, also happen to be football lovers.

But some of these little groups—and the venues where they gather—could use Prig's help. They need his dollars, but more than that, they need his energy.

Face it, Professor. You live here. So be here. This is a more interesting (and less idyllic) place than those out-of-town reporters gave it credit for being. It can be more interesting still.

Ten Things to Be Thankful For

NOVEMBER 27, 2014

Time to tally up the gratitudes, this being Thanksgiving week. In the order in which they popped into my head:

1. Think of all the natural disasters we're not likely to get clobbered by here in Happy Valley: earthquakes, tsunamis, typhoons, cyclones, sandstorms, volcanoes, avalanches, wildfires. Which means we probably won't host the friendly folks from FEMA—also a good thing.

   If the Ten Plagues were going to be visited upon us—blood, frogs, gnats, boils, etc., they probably would have been dispatched in fall of 2011. Or was that what the satellite TV trucks were all about?

   True, we could get a blizzard like the ones they've just gotten in western New York. We're bound to get an ice storm. Maybe a Polar Vortex Redux (not to bring back bad memories, but we had a low of negative nine degrees last January and a high of six). And come thunderstorm season, some of our basements will be under water.

   But it is exquisitely beautiful here in May and October, and there are far muggier and buggier places in July and August.

2. Rush hours hereabouts are more like rush half-hours. In Atlanta, I hear, "rush hour" can last from 6:30 to 11:00 A.M. and from 3:30 to 7:00 P.M. On the other hand, there are those long lines at the Creamery.

3. People complain about how cloudy this place is—many's the time I've left New York on a clear day and enjoyed a sunlit

drive through such Garden State garden spots as Netcong and Allamuchy and on into the Poconos, only to descend into the gray zone that is Central Pennsylvania—but clouds doth lovely sunsets make. We get stunners here.

4. They've shed their leaves, alas, but magnificent trees abound, especially on the Penn State campus. I've even learned to admire their bones in winter. And I think the people who designed the H.O. Smith Botanic Gardens deserve more recognition than they've gotten. Their handiwork is sublime.

5. It is now possible to get decent bread, Thai food, and locally brewed beer here. This was not the case back in the twentieth century.

6. The last few times I've gone out of town and told someone I teach at Penn State, they've responded with sympathy rather than scorn. I guess that's progress. Of course, these are people I'm introduced to at parties and other polite gatherings. I hear it's a different story when you're out and about in a Penn State hoodie.

7. When was the last time you went out to a movie or a meal and didn't run into someone you know? Some people find this aspect of small-town life claustrophobic. I like it, even if it sometimes leads to a forty-five-minute chat around the potato bins in Wegmans. As Gertrude Stein said, "I am I because my little dog knows me."

8. The steady stream of students makes this place about as recession-proof as a place can be. That's why, they say, this place was called Happy Valley. I suppose if tuition keeps rising, American families may one day rise up and decide they're not getting their money's worth from these universities and get their kids ready for the workforce in some other fashion. Then, too, it's possible higher-ed will go all-online in the not-too-distant future, and these stately campuses with their beautiful trees and lawns will become retirement communities. That would be convenient for geezers-in-waiting like me.

9. Speakers, readings, concerts, films—nightly, practically. Just in the past couple of weeks, I went to an international poetry night at Webster's, two documentary screenings at the State

Theatre, a touring production of "Much Ado About Nothing" on campus, and a talk/photo presentation on fracking at the Palmer Museum. We bring in an amazing number of smart, talented people, but more than ever, I'm also appreciating that there are an amazing number of smart, talented people who live here.

10. It is often said that we live in the middle of nowhere and are equally inaccessible from everywhere, but in the last couple of weeks we have had visitors who were driving from Pittsburgh to New York and from Chicago to New York. We're a veritable crossroads!

There. That's ten. I could probably think of more, but, well, fond as I am of State College, I'm spending the holiday in California (where it's going to be in the mid-sixties for the next few days), so hey, gotta fly.

Savor that meal, friends, and more than that, savor the people you share it with.

Who's Naked Now?

MARCH 24, 2015

What makes discovery of Kappa Delta Rho's top-secret Facebook page so distressing is that it constitutes hard evidence of long-suspected behaviors and attitudes.

Here is photographic proof (unless it's an elaborate hoax) that when women pass out at fraternity parties, the guys don't take care of them.

They take advantage of them.

Reaction, predictably, has ranged along a continuum from "a few bad apples" at one end, to "tip of the iceberg" at the other.

The "bad apples" defense rings hollow at the moment. There seem to be a few too many bad apples.

When we hear that photos have been taken of women who were undressed and unconscious and that those photos were then posted on social media, we don't want to hear the usual high-minded hooey about the brothers' dedication to service, leadership, academic achievement, and brotherhood.

We don't want them to deflect blame onto a scandal-mongering media system that has it in for fraternities and Penn State.

We want them to condemn such behaviors and attitudes in the strongest possible terms. We want them to implement changes in the orientation of new members and the planning of social events to curtail such behaviors and attitudes. We want to see a sense of urgency.

Instead, we have Greek "leadership" counseling restraint until all the facts are known—fair enough—and attempting to muzzle the rank and file lest anyone stray from the party line in an interview with one of those odious reporters.

And we have an anonymous KDR member reminding readers of *Philadelphia* magazine that Greeks are the prime fundraisers and organizers of Dance Marathon.

Overall message: this is first and foremost a public relations problem. Now where in the world could they have learned that?

As laudable as THON is—who can fault an activity that raises $13 million "for the kids?"—its cynical invocation as a damage control tool is hard to stomach.

THON is a new suit, a shave, and a haircut on an accused felon. Ladies and gentlemen of the jury, does this choirboy look like an ax murderer to you?

THON is regular Sunday church attendance by someone who lies, cheats, and steals the other six days of the week.

THON is the fig leaf that is supposed to cover every shameful incident at the stately mansions with the Greek letters on the lintel.

Brothers of the fifty fraternities at this mighty university, I'm sure you engage in many fine and noble pursuits, but this is no time for sanctimony.

As in 2011, the work that needs to be done at Penn State goes way beyond image repair. A wholesale examination of the pathologies of undergraduate life, and the outsized role played by fraternities—and alcohol—in those pathologies, is called for.

President Barron says he's forming a task force. Well and good. But don't look for immediate or dramatic changes, given the powerful interests involved.

Those who advocate "tearing down" KDR, for example, must reckon with the fact that the university doesn't own the building and needs the student housing—as well as the donations from fraternity alumni with happy memories of their own loutish undergraduate exploits.

Then too, if men have always behaved like swine toward women—especially, the anonymous expert who spoke to *Philly* Mag might have added, drunken men under the age of twenty-two living in unsupervised sex-segregated groups—it's not going to be easy to make them see the error of their ways.

But what if they gave a party and nobody came?

If fraternity houses are not safe places for women, perhaps the quickest way to change the culture is to reject it.

I know this sounds like victim blaming: it isn't the women who should have to alter their behavior; it's the men. But I'm thinking in practical terms: women can change the social dynamic at Penn State starting this weekend just by not showing up—or showing up with picket signs.

I ran my boycott idea past the sorority members in one of my classes the other day. They didn't like it. They didn't think it was fair to single out the fraternities as the locus of Penn State's rape culture. So I asked them if they felt safe at fraternity parties.

Oh the cluelessness of the middle-aged man. If you're a woman, they explained, you don't feel safe anywhere around here. Going to a fraternity party is no different from going to an apartment party: you have to have your wits about you, and you have to take care of each other.

I couldn't argue, though I thought this was a rather grim mindset to bring to one's leisure activities, and that the sorority sisters were a little too implicated in Greek culture to challenge it.

As one who lived two doors down from KDR for sixteen years, I'll say this for my former neighbors: I doubt they're a whole lot worse than the house on the corner, or the one across the street, or the ones at the University of Oklahoma.

Apples vs. Icebergs: Who's Right?

APRIL 1, 2015

I want to return to the dueling "bad apples" vs. "tip of the iceberg" perspectives on the photos of unconscious and unclad women that were posted on a Penn State fraternity's Facebook page.

Apples and Icebergs agree on one thing: the taking and posting of such photos is despicable.

Where they differ is in their sense of whether the Kappa Delta Rho members' actions are indicative of a larger problem.

Apples take a narrowly legalistic approach: Punish those who committed crimes. Don't condemn all Greeks.

Icebergs take a broadly cultural approach. When multiple members of a group commit similar outrages, be they football players, cops, fraternity brothers, or university administrators, it makes sense to ask whether their behavior reflects the group's ethos.

Last week, Jay Paterno wrote that "we must not fall into the trap of believing that an individual's acts are always a reflection of the group that person belongs to, or of some 'culture' fostered by that group."

Paterno's an Apple. I agree with his "always": certainly there are plenty of individuals who act in ways that are totally at odds with the values of their culture. Any statement that begins with "all"—all white cops are racists, all Penn Staters care more about football than about protecting kids from a child molester, all Greeks are sexual predators—is probably going to be false.

But we humans are cultural creatures, through and through. From babyhood on, we imitate the people around us. As we mature, we begin to choose our influences, which is to say, we join subcultures. With group membership comes a vocabulary, a style, a set of ritualized behaviors, a worldview.

Even "nonconformists"—goths, hipsters, skinheads, and the like—conform. We wouldn't recognize individuals as members of those subcultures if they didn't.

Apples caution against guilt by association and rushes to judgment. They call for restraint until the facts are known. They challenge sweeping generalizations that are unsupported by data.

But data, say the Icebergs, can only tell us so much.

Take sexual assaults. At this writing, the *Daily Collegian*'s running count of reported assaults since the start of the spring semester stands at twenty. Considered as a percentage of all the human interactions that have occurred in State College since January, that's a tiny number.

Most women have not been sexually assaulted. Most men have not committed sexual assaults. That is true even if we factor in the unknown number of sexual assaults that have not been reported.

It's easy to brand the sexual predators in our midst as sociopathic outliers and absolve everyone else of all responsibility. But Icebergs ask whether those who are committing sexual assaults are absorbing messages from the subculture of which they are members that say there is nothing wrong with having sex with someone who is too drunk to consent.

If that's a norm, you have a culture of rape. If 144 members and former members of a fraternity are entertained by a Facebook page that displays photos that never should have been taken, that too, suggests, if not a culture of rape, then certainly a culture that condones the mistreatment of women.

When we turn our attention from legal culpability to moral responsibility, things become more complicated than separating the guilty from the innocent. To cite an obvious example, responsibility for the Holocaust lies not just with those who carried out Hitler's orders, but with everyone on both sides of the Atlantic who looked the other way.

The famous Edmund Burke quote applies: "The only thing necessary for the triumph of evil is for good men to do nothing."

To say that the group should not be blamed for the misdeeds of the individual is to dodge the question of how the group's norms, or even its silences, enable the miscreant.

At the State Theatre last week, Caitlin Flanagan, the writer of a scathing piece on fraternities for the *Atlantic* last year, called fraternities an anachronism. In an age of diversity, she said, they remain bastions of race and gender segregation. We tend to admire adherence to tradition, but a lot of Greek traditions—exclusion, hazing, dubiously consensual drunken sex—are pretty nasty.

Knowing how entrenched fraternities are, Flanagan suggested that it might be more fruitful to attack the real problem bedeviling universities: alcohol abuse.

When an audience member said the drinking culture was likewise too entrenched to dislodge, Flanagan recalled that people said much the same thing when cigarettes were found to be a health hazard. Yet millions of people quit smoking.

Binge drinking and dubiously consensual sex have become cultural norms on college campuses. But cultural norms can change.

Battle of the Bamboo

MAY 20, 2015

What I need is a giant panda, though a troop of lemurs would do.

But until the borough of State College relaxes its ban on the keeping of large exotic animals, it's going to just be me and my loppers, waging a lonely battle against the yummy bamboo along my back fence.

Now I have nothing against bamboo. I like the way the word bamboo sounds like the music made by a bamboo flute. I can play the Dave Van Ronk song ("You take a stick of bamboo, you take a stick of bamboo . . .") on guitar (only two chords!).

And now that I have my very own bamboo grove, I appreciate the way it screens our house from our neighbors on the next block, whom I have never seen.

But remember how you barely survived the frigid winter of 2014–15? My bamboo didn't fare so well either.

At first, I was going to leave it alone and see if it came back to life. Then I noticed that those folks at the Hosbog (the H.O. Smith Botanic Gardens), who gave us a glorious explosion of tulips this spring (gone now, alas), had razed their bamboo grove. And then, a week or two later I saw that the baby bamboo shoots were already two or three feet high.

You always hear about how fast bamboo grows, but it's astonishing to see it actually happening. In the growth-friendly month of May at least, it seems possible to stare at bamboo for an hour and watch it get taller, as if you were watching time-elapsed photography.

Indeed, if the Wikipedia entry is to be trusted, bamboo has been known to grow as fast as ninety-eight inches in twenty-four hours. That's a little scary. I can imagine a time in the not-too-distant future when what began as a little clump of bamboo in my yard becomes the Great Bamboo Forest that covers the area of Central Pennsylvania where a town and a university once stood.

Or as a friend warned me, if you don't trim it back, don't be surprised if you come downstairs some morning and see your bamboo in your kitchen, pouring itself a cup of coffee.

Thus reassured, sort of, that my bamboo curtain would quickly reestablish itself, I asked one of the Hosboggers how to go about thinning the grove. Her recommendation: go at it with a small chainsaw.

This was not the response I expected or was hoping for. I'll be frank (so to speak): I don't like chainsaws. It mostly has to do with the fact that I am morbidly noise averse, though I also find it entirely too easy to picture a chainsaw separating me from various important body parts as easily as a knife goes through room-temperature butter.

And I've never even seen any of the installments of "The Texas Chainsaw Massacre" franchise.

(Lest you think all of us professorial types are wimpy noodles, I'll have you know that I once read a book about cutting firewood. No, no, I'm kidding. I actually went out in the woods with a chainsaw back in my Northern California Mountain Man days. And yes, it did warm me twice. Maybe better the first time, which is the problem with heating with wood.)

Ignoring the advice of the professionals (as is my wont), I decided to see what would happen if I brought a nasty pair of loppers to bear on the task at hand. At the hardware store I picked out the ones that looked most like a snapping turtle on steroids.

I noticed as I made my way to the check stand that the nice people who were purchasing petunias, pansies, and peonies were eyeballing me warily, glancing first at the fearsome bamboo slayer in my hands and then up at my face, as if to gauge whether I was the sort of person who would commit mayhem in a small-town hardware store.

They gave me a wide berth. Call me Lopperface.

When I got home, I dove into the grove and commenced to lop. At first I felt vindicated. My loppers worked great on bamboo—like butter.

But I grossly underestimated the Sispheanicity of the job. All day Saturday I lopped 'til I dropped, and as I sit here gazing upon my handiwork, I can't see as I've even made a dent.

This is not, by the way, an as-you-soweth-even-so-shall-ye-reapeth situation. I sowethed not. The bamboo has lived here longer than I have—just so my neighbors know, before the bamboo starts inviting itself into their kitchens for coffee.

Clearly, I should have rented a chainsaw. Better still, I should have hired someone—which is the conclusion I usually come to when I'm in over my head on a home maintenance project.

Or perhaps I should invite a panda over for lunch.

To Weed, or Not to Weed

JULY 15, 2015

When it comes to weeds, everyone's a philosopher.

Several times now, I with my black thumb have asked green-thumbed friends to help me sort out the riot of vegetation that is threatening to engulf my house.

I'm not asking them to contribute any stoop labor.

I just want them to tiptoe through the jungle with me and say, "This one's a weed, that one's an ornamental grass, and that's ground-cover," so I'll know what to pull and what to leave in peace.

Instead, I get these impromptu TED talks:

"What, after all, is a weed?" they muse.

The thesis of these horticultural philosophers echoes the Wikipedia entry on the subject, which defines a weed as "a plant considered undesirable in a particular situation, 'a plant in the wrong place.'"

If you think a plant is pretty, the philosophers tell me, keep it. If you think it's ugly, yank it.

I suppose I should be grateful for this kind of advice. I'm being told that there's no right answer, that I can use my own judgment.

My students hate when I tell them there is no right answer, and now I see why. When you lack confidence in your own judgment, you don't want to be told to exercise it. You just want to be told what to do.

Here is what happens when my wife and I use our own judgment in the garden: She, working on one side of the driveway, will rip out a plant that she thinks is a weed. I, working on the other side of the driveway, will leave the same plant undisturbed, thinking it's groundcover.

This is wholly in keeping with her tendency to get rid of stuff and my tendency to hang onto stuff. Just the other day she held up a tangle of thin wires she found in the shed.

"What are these?" she asked.

"Old guitar strings," I said. "I thought they might be useful for something."

She couldn't imagine what they could be useful for. Truth be told, neither could I.

One of the few weeds I feel confident pulling is the dandelion, because of its readily identifiable yellow crown and its lion-tooth leaves (hence its French name, dent-de-lion—pronounced, roughly, Don d'Lee Owen).

I even have a special dandelion-pulling tool that looks like a pogo stick, and requires no stooping. But I get flak for using it, on aesthetic and gastronomic grounds.

Dandelions are pretty, say the aesthetes. Why pull them?

Dandelions are tasty, say the gastronomes. If you're going to pull 'em, eat 'em.

I have trouble eating a thing that was held in such contempt by the suburban dads of my childhood, even when it goes by its French name. I have the same problem with escargot.

Now that dandelion season is mostly over, I have set my sights on a nasty, spiny-looking thing, which I believe is a Canada thistle. One of its nicknames, fittingly, is the Lettuce from Hell.

The thing about fighting a spiny weed: it fights back. Right through my gardening gloves.

When I get tired of battling the Lettuce from Hell, I go after the Virginia creeper. What's fun about pulling this plant is that it makes me feel like a character in a war movie who stumbles on a trip wire, which, when he starts yanking on it, leads to an explosive device fifty feet away.

Virginia creeper is the boa constrictor of the vegetable kingdom. In one corner of my backyard I found its tendrils coiled so tightly around a tree branch that it was impossible to separate them.

Fiendish as it looked, the vine didn't seem to be hurting the tree any, but when I did my research, I learned that the creeper's leaves can indeed deprive the host tree of sunlight.

On the other hand, the VC's leaves turn an attractive shade of burgundy in the fall, and it is therefore popular as an ornamental plant.

See how hard it is to decide what a weed is? Apart from the Canada thistle, I don't find any of the plants in my garden ugly in and of themselves. Together, though, they form a tableau of neglect that makes me feel vaguely ashamed.

Thus have I been spending entirely too many evening and weekend hours rooting around in my flower beds. A moment may soon arrive when I feel about weeding the way I have long felt about shaving: it is an unnatural, even a violent act, to scrape off the hair that grows on a man's face.

Stuff grows. Let it.

I don't like the look of an over-tended garden any more than I like the look of an over-groomed person.

I do, however, want to be able to get to my front door without using a machete.

In Search of the Cure for the Summertime Blues

AUGUST 19, 2015

I should like August more than I do.

It's my birthday month, for one thing. (My astrological sign is Vertigo: we're so analytical, we make other people's heads spin.)

It's also a month when my coats, scarves, and gloves remain hidden away in the attic like batty relatives until I let them out at Thanksgiving.

Above all, it's a month when, as a member of the professoriate, I am not required to be in any particular place at any particular time, at least for the first three weeks (though I'm writing day and night, honest!).

So what's not to like, as my grandmother used to say.

Well, you know how stripy-leaved hostas have started to look tired—bug-nibbled, not as taut, not as intensely green as they were earlier in the summer?

The way they look is the way I feel. The thrill of shedding sweaters and socks has worn off. The thrill of being sprung from the classroom and the office, incredibly, has also worn off.

I ought, then, to be happy: Here comes the new academic year! Here comes fall! Woohoo!

Instead, I feel that age-old and ageless human dread of the end of summer and the coming of winter. This has less to do with my unreadiness for the fall semester—I love my job, honest!—than with my annual disappointment in what I accomplished over the summer.

I charge into June with big plans. I'm going to produce enough scholarship to get me enshrined in the Egghead Hall of Fame.

I'm going to rejigger my finances in such a way that I can retire tomorrow, if I want to, with enough money stashed away to support me until my one hundredth birthday.

I'm going to make enough home improvements to double the resale value of my house.

Instead, I spend entire days fussing with one stupid paragraph, blow so much dough that I may not make it to my next birthday, never mind my one hundredth, and do more damage to house and garden than I undo.

(Just the other day I tried to separate a belt from a pair of pants hanging on a hook and succeeding only in yanking down the board the hook was affixed to, along with all the other hooks and items of clothing suspended therefrom.)

So now comes the magical thinking stage of summer. In the next three days I'm going to do all the work that I meant to get done over the past three months.

Just as soon as this baseball game is over. Oh, and I haven't done the crossword puzzle yet.

I'm wise to such stalling tactics. Every semester I have a few students who fall hopelessly behind. I urge them to drop the class before it's too late to get any of their tuition dollars back. They swear they will devote the weekend ahead to a marathon catch-up session. Experience has taught me to be deeply skeptical.

See, this is the problem with August. I haven't even finished tweaking my syllabi and I'm already thinking about the late drop date.

I vented my disenchantment with the current month to a friend, who had a ready explanation.

"August," he said, "is like one long Sunday night."

A young friend in New York considered this formulation, and elaborated on it:

"June is Friday," she said, "July is Saturday and August is Sunday."

When I ran these day-month analogies by a colleague, he told me he associates Sundays not with football or feasting or family outings, but with the tick-tick-tick of the "60 Minutes" stopwatch on Sunday night TV.

Thus does our accursed inability to live in the moment rear its head. Not only does knowing that tomorrow is Monday detract from our enjoyment of Sunday, but knowing next month is September detracts from our enjoyment of August.

You old-timers will remember a square, purple book popular in the 1970s. Yeah, that one: *Be Here Now*, by Ram Dass (the former Dr. Richard Alpert, who dropped acid with Timothy Leary at Harvard before he went to India and decided that meditation and yoga offered a better path to enlightenment than hallucinogenic drugs).

Perhaps my way of being here now is to watch baseball and solve crosswords.

If so, I only look like I'm wasting time. In fact, I am journeying beyond dread, beyond course preps, beyond citation indices, beyond retirement accounts, beyond hardware and software, beyond August, to the eternal present, where the pitcher is always rocking into his windup, and the answer to 14-Across is just about to pop into my otherwise spotless mind.

Don't Be Rattled

SEPTEMBER 2, 2015

Not to alarm you would-be woods walkers, but there are rattlesnakes out there.

We met one the other day, all curled up along the John Wert Trail, which follows tea-colored Sinking Creek away from Bear Meadows, deep in the Rothrock State Forest.

A timber rattler this was, thick as a baguette.

There were five of us. Louise told us that, according to local lore in South Africa, where she's from, the first person alerts the snake, the second person irritates the snake, and the third person gets bitten.

Happily, Rosa did not alert, Louise did not irritate, Dorn did not get bitten, and my wife and I did not have to spring into heroic action—a good thing because we would not have known what to do.

Perhaps, I suggested, we should review best practices in the event that we alert and irritate some other snake as we make our wary way back to the car.

We had heard contradictory things: Suck the venom out of the wound. Cut away the area around the puncture (none of us had a knife). Apply a tourniquet. Ice it (no ice, either).

Then: Get to a hospital, pronto. No, stay still while your companions rush out and get help.

I was reminded of the conflicting advice I'd heard about what to do in an encounter with a bear. Do you:

(a) Lie down, play dead, and hope the bear cops a sniff and a cheap feel?

(b) Run like hell or, if you're nimble enough, climb a tree?

(c) Stand your ground, inform the bear in the strongest possible terms that you are not to be trifled with, and chuck rocks or brandish a stick?

Bonus question: how about if it's a mountain lion rather than a bear?

Hereabouts, the only mountain lion you're likely to meet is the one in the Penn State jersey at sporting events and pep rallies, but in California I was told that if a lion gets up in your grille, gouge his eyes out.

This made me fervently hope I would never encounter a cougar in the wild.

One may, however meet a black bear in Penn's Woods. I met one in my backyard once, three blocks from downtown State College. (We had blueberry bushes.)

For that matter, I remember a news story about a bear in the tree outside the florist shop on Allen Street. (The police complained that some bystanders were unhelpfully baiting the bear. A human was cited for disorderly conduct. The bear was tranked and released into the wild.)

There are two things to keep in mind when you have a close encounter with a black bear. One is that the first thought that pops into its head when it sees a human is not "Chow time!" We may be tasty, but we are not a normal part of a bear's fare.

The other thing to keep in mind is that we are imposing creatures in our own right: they would prefer not to mess with us.

For these two reasons, black bear encounters rarely turn ugly. When they do, the experts say, it's usually because you've gotten between them and their cubbies or between them and their yummies.

(When I was a reporter in California, there were occasional stories of visitors posing with adorable bear cubs, then being charged by the momma, who apparently did not fancy her little ones being treated as teddy bears.)

If a bear encounter does turn hostile, try talking to the bear calmly first, the experts say. You know, explain that you are a sincere man from the land where the palm trees grow and assure him that a bearskin rug would clash mightily with the décor of your living room.

If that doesn't work, raise holy hell and throw stuff.

Oh, and use your bear spray—which means you should probably carry bear spray. (I never have.)

As for rattlesnakes: forget "Guantanamera." They feel the vibrations of your footfalls rather than hear your crooning. Like bears, they're unlikely to strike unless startled. So don't startle them.

OK, if you do startle a rattler—easy to do, it seems to me, because they have this nice camo thing going—and you're struck, the experts want you to remain calm.

Yeah, good luck with that.

Also: no tourniquet, no suction, no cutting, no ice.

Some of the experts say to stay put, which doesn't seem all that compatible with getting to a hospital if you're on the trail and far from your car.

Those that acknowledge this inconvenient fact advise walking out slowly and resting frequently. The idea is to keep your heart rate down so the poison doesn't circulate.

The good news: assuming you get treatment, rattlesnake venom is unlikely to kill you.

The better news: once people read this column, you'll have the woods all to yourself.

It's Wonderful to Be Here, It's Certainly a Thrill

OCTOBER 14, 2015

It was twenty years ago today: I rolled into State College in a car I no longer drive, to move into a house I no longer own, and work for a newspaper chain that no longer exists.

I was the father of three young children and the scruffy human of a scruffy mutt named Bop the Movie Dog, an easterner glad to be back in the land of fireflies and fall foliage after two decades in California.

Now the kids are grown, the Bopster has gone to the great kennel in the sky, and I'm asking myself, did I mean to stay here this long?

To tell you the truth, I don't remember.

I know that we moved to State College, in part, because it seemed like a good place to raise a family.

I know that we didn't want to shuffle the kids in and out of schools. With the youngest still in diapers, that meant we figured to settle in—unless we hated the place.

We didn't hate it.

. . . .

This is a sweet spot in many ways. Lots of trees, easy access to green space, pretty campus, stimulating events, stimulating people.

I don't love it unreservedly, however. Too far from the sea. Too far from the bright lights of Broadway.

If State College were small but close to Gotham, its smallness would be part of its appeal: one could nip out for a jolt of big-city buzz, then zip back to the ease of small-town life.

If State College were remote and large, there would be enough here to hold one's interest.

For me, in other words, small and remote is not a great combo. Or, more accurately, it's a fine combo for a month or so at a time. Then I need to get the hell out of here.

If I don't, I start to feel like I'm trapped in a trash compactor, like the "Star Wars" heroes. I know that I am fortunate that, like Luke Skywalker and friends, I can escape before the walls meet.

With the small-and-remote problem thus solved, it is entirely possible that I will retire here, and stay until I go to the great news-room in the sky.

There are worse fates.

....

As a twenty-year man, I have been in Happy Valley longer than the Bryce Jordan Center, Medlar Field, Wegman's, the H.O. Smith Botanic Gardens, and the IST Building.

I remember old Schlow, the old HUB, the old municipal building, and the old Creamery.

Why, I remember when Beaver Stadium held only ninety-four thousand people. It was so quiet you could hear a vuvuzela being blown directly into your bad ear.

In fact, I was there the day JoePa got on the PA system to encourage fans to throw snowballs at the Michigan players—I mean, to order the fans to quit pelting the poor Wolverines.

And I was in the old Creamery to report on the scandal that almost ended Bill Clinton's presidency. No, not his affair with "that woman." I'm talking about his claiming executive privilege to mix ice cream flavors.

(It pains me to add that I was also on the scene to report on the sniper who killed one student and wounded another as they crossed the HUB lawn.)

When I got to town, there were still phone booths in the HUB, and you could still drive through campus on Shortlidge Road.

I was here for the fights over traffic barriers in College Heights, a Hooter's on East College Avenue, and a second high school in the State College Area School District.

I shopped at O.W. Houtz, dined at the Hummingbird Room, and read magazines with a side of Chunky Monkey at much-missed Graham's on Allen Street.

I also recall when there were two single-screen theaters downtown and no multiplex on North Atherton; when you could browse for rentals at Blockbuster or Hollywood, or catch a movie at the Starlite Drive-In; and when the State Theatre was waiting for a savior.

And speaking of saviors, I remember when Penn State had a football coach who walked on water, a president who played the washboard, and a professor who smoked dope in a lawn chair on College Avenue.

. . . .

In the twenty years I have been here, I have known people who totally buy into the Happy Valley mythos.

I have also known people who feel trapped in Zombie Nation, or as I like to call it, the Land of the Woo People.

But as an on-the-one-hand/but-on-the-other-hand kind of guy, I compare thee, Happy Valley, to a bed topped by a fluffy blanket.

Sometimes I feel all comfy and cozy here.

Sometimes I feel like I'm suffocating.

And sometimes I feel like my friends and I are making blanket forts, eating popcorn, and having the greatest sleepover ever.